MULTICULTURAL EDUCATION SERIES

James A. Banks, Series Editor

For a complete list of series titles, please visit www.tcpr   *continued)*

T0383990

THE CIVIL RIGHTS ROAD TO DEEPER LEARNING

FIVE ESSENTIALS FOR EQUITY

Kia Darling-Hammond and
Linda Darling-Hammond

Foreword by Eliza Byard

TEACHERS COLLEGE PRESS

TEACHERS COLLEGE | COLUMBIA UNIVERSITY
NEW YORK AND LONDON

Published by Teachers College Press,® 1234 Amsterdam Avenue, New York, NY 10027

Copyright © 2022 by Teachers College, Columbia University

Front cover painting: Jacob Lawrence, *Migration Series No.58: In the North the African American had more educational opportunities*, 1941. © 2022 The Jacob and Gwendolyn Knight Lawrence Foundation, Seattle / Artists Rights Society (ARS), New York.

Library of Congress Cataloging-in-Publication Data is available at loc.gov

ISBN 978-0-8077-6722-1 (paper)
ISBN 978-0-8077-6723-8 (hardcover)
ISBN 978-0-8077-8116-6 (ebook)

Printed on acid-free paper
Manufactured in the United States of America

Contents

Series Foreword

In this eloquently written, compelling, timely, and incisive book, Kia Darling-Hammond and Linda Darling-Hammond maintain that equal educational opportunity is a civil right and that many students, because of their social-class, racial, ethnic, and linguistics characteristics, are not given the learning opportunities that will enable them to attain the *deeper learning* essential for functioning in a diverse global world and workforce. The knowledge and skills that comprise deeper learning have been provided historically in U.S. schools only to a small elite group of students who were presumed to be the future leaders of the nation. Because of the global and technologically mediated world in which we now live, all students need to acquire the knowledge and skills that comprise deeper learning, which consists of six competencies: (1) mastering core academic content, (2) thinking critically and solving complex problems, (3) communicating effectively, (4) working collaboratively, (5) learning how to learn, and (6) developing academic mindsets. The authors write, "There is still a long road to travel to access deeper learning for many students, and the destination will depend in substantial part on high-quality education being acknowledged as a right for all" (p. 82.).

Kia Darling-Hammond and Linda Darling-Hammond believe that it will be a difficult and fraught journey to implement deeper learning for all students because of the structural, racial, and social-class inequalities that exist within U.S. society and schools, including those related to school funding, the toxic environmental and health inequalities that many low-income and students of color experience, and the quality of teachers and teaching in many low-income minoritized communities. In most schools in which low-income students (more than 1 in 5 students in the United States live in poverty) and students of color are majorities, the focus is not on teaching critical thinking skills but on teaching lower-level facts that are presumed to help students perform successfully on standardized tests. Students of color and special education students are also suspended or expelled at much higher rates than White middle-class students, which contributes to their lower academic achievement and social problems in school.

This informative, practical, and engaging book explicates how schools can be reformed to facilitate deeper learning by students from diverse racial, ethnic, social-class, and linguistic groups. It describes why a safe and healthy community is needed for effective learning to take place in schools, why school systems need to be well funded and resourced, why educators need to create safe and inclusive learning environments, and why high-quality teaching and a high-quality curriculum are essential for students from myriad groups to attain deeper learning. Policymakers, teachers, and other school practitioners will find this book practical and helpful. It is undergirded not only by strong theoretical explanations and empirical data but also contains practical and vivid examples of school and curriculum interventions, such as lessons exemplifying deeper learning in a 4th-grade classroom in New York City; and a 9th- and 10th-grade biology class in a San Francisco school. Teachers will be able to adapt many of the teaching examples described in this book to their classrooms. The teaching examples in this book also describe ingenious ways for teachers to incorporate student cultural elements and home languages into their instruction and ways to make their teaching culturally responsive (Gay, 2010) and culturally sustaining (Paris, 2012). School, college, and university faculty will find descriptions of interventions such as the Comer School Development Program (SDP), designed to enhance academic achievement and social development for elementary school students, and the Teacher Residency Model and Marshall Plan for Teaching, designed to reform teacher education, useful for envisioning and planning effective change strategies.

The focus of this book on reforming schools in ways that will facilitate deeper learning for students from diverse groups is an original and significant contribution to the Multicultural Education Series. The major purpose of the Multicultural Education Series is to provide preservice educators, practicing educators, graduate students, scholars, and policymakers with an interrelated and comprehensive set of books that summarizes and analyzes important research, theory, and practice related to the education of ethnic, racial, cultural, and linguistic groups in the United States and the education of mainstream students about diversity. The dimensions of multicultural education, developed by Banks and described in the *Handbook of Research on Multicultural Education* (Banks, 2004), *The Routledge International Companion to Multicultural Education* (Banks, 2009), and in the *Encyclopedia of Diversity in Education* (Banks, 2012), provide the conceptual framework for the development of the publications in the Series. The dimensions are content integration, the knowledge construction process, prejudice reduction, equity pedagogy, and an empowering institutional culture and social structure. The books in the Multicultural Education Series provide research, theoretical, and practical knowledge about the behaviors and learning characteristics of students of color (Conchas & Vigil, 2012; Lee, 2007), language minority students (Gándara & Hopkins, 2010; Valdés, 2001; Valdés al., 2011), low-income students (Cookson, 2013; Gorski, 2018), multiracial youth (Joseph & Briscoe-Smith, 2021; Mahiri, 2017); and other minoritized population groups, such as students who speak different varieties of English (Charity Hudley & Mallinson, 2011), and LGBTQ youth (Mayo, 2022).

An important implicit message of this book is that institutional and structural racism is a factor that negatively affects the opportunities for students of color to acquire deeper learning. Other books in the Multicultural Education Series that focus on *institutional and structural racism* and ways to reduce it include Özlem

Sensoy and Robin DiAngelo (2017), *Is Everyone Really Equal? An Introduction to Key Concepts in Social Justice Education* (Second Edition); Gary Howard (2016), *We Can't Teach What Do Don't Know: White Teachers, Multiracial Schools* (Third Edition); Zeus Leonardo (2013), *Race Frameworks: A Multidimensional Theory of Racism and Education*; Daniel Solórzano and Lindsay Pérez Huber (2020), *Racial Microaggressions: Using Critical Race Theory to Respond to Everyday Racism*; and Gloria Ladson-Billings (2021), *Critical Race Theory in Education: A Scholar's Journey.*

This book describes myriad ways in which the quests for and attainment of civil rights expands equal educational opportunities for African American and other students of color. Citing the work of economist Rucker Johnson, the authors describe why desegregated schools result in higher academic achievement for all students. They write, "Desegregation results in overall academic gains for students, in part because low-poverty, predominantly White schools are typically better resourced than segregated schools serving students of color" (p. 11). Students of color in desegregated schools have higher academic achievement, which includes "higher graduation rates and stronger wages, less poverty, and lower incarceration as adults" (p. 11). The authors also describe the ways in which the federal government, the U.S. Supreme Court, and local school districts have abandoned the quest for racially desegregated schools since the 1980s, which was epitomized in the 2007 Supreme Court decision in *Parents Involved in Community Schools v. Seattle School District No. 1.* This decision, which was supported by the George W. Bush administration, sanctioned the end of school desegregation in the Seattle Public Schools. A report by the Economic Policy Institute indicates that African American children are five times more likely than White children (69.2% vs. 12.9%) to attend schools that are highly segregated by race and ethnicity (Garcia, 2020). The authors call schools that serve more than 90% students of color from low-income families "apartheid schools." These schools "typically also feature a revolving door of unprepared teachers whose lack of training and high attrition rates depress students' achievement levels further" (p. 30).

This erudite, trenchant, and engaging book contains a gold mine of empirical data and information that will help school leaders, policymakers, teachers, and other school practitioners to transform schools and communities in ways that will enable students from myriad cultural, ethnic, and racial groups to attain deeper learning and become more effective and contributing citizens of the nation. I am pleased to welcome this book to the Multicultural Education Series, which is the third book that Linda Darling-Hammond has contributed to the Series and the first by Kia Darling-Hammond, whom I am pleased to welcome as a Series author. Linda's other two books in the Series are *Learning to Teach for Social Justice*, edited with Jennifer French and Silvia Paloma Garcia-Lopez (2002); and *The Flat World and Education: How America's Commitment to Equity Will Determine our Future* (Darling-Hammond, 2010). This best-selling book received the coveted Grawemeyer Award in Education in 2012.

I am pleased to publish this book in the Multicultural Education Series for both personal and professional reasons. Linda Darling-Hammond is not only one of the most eloquent, prolific, and influential scholars writing on education today, she is also a valued friend and colleague who has for decades supported my work and the field of multicultural education at pivotal points, for which I shall always be grateful.

—James A. Banks

REFERENCES

Banks, J. A. (2004). Multicultural education: Historical development, dimensions, and practice. In J. A. Banks & C. A. M. Banks (Eds.), *Handbook of research on multicultural education* (pp. 3–29). Jossey-Bass.

Banks, J. A. (Ed.). (2009). *The Routledge international companion to multicultural education*. Routledge.

Banks, J. A. (2012). Multicultural education: Dimensions of. In J. A. Banks (Ed), *Encyclopedia of diversity in education* (vol. 3, pp. 1538–1547). Sage Publications.

Charity Hudley, A. H., & Mallinson, C. (2011). *Understanding language variation in U. S. schools*. Teachers College Press.

Conchas, G. Q., & Vigil, J. D. (2012). *Streetsmart schoolsmart: Urban poverty and the education of adolescent boys*. Teachers College Press.

Cookson, P. W., Jr. (2013). *Class rules: Exposing inequality in American high schools*. Teachers College Press.

Darling-Hammond, L. (2010). *The flat world and education: How America's commitment to equity will determine our future*. Teachers College Press.

Darling-Hammond, L., French, J., & García-Lopez, S. P. (Eds.). (2002). *Learning to teach for social justice*. Teachers College Press.

Gándara, P., & Hopkins, M. (Eds.). (2010). *Forbidden language: English language learners and restrictive language policies*. Teachers College Press.

Garcia, E. (2020, February1). Schools are still segregated, and Black children are paying a price. *Economic Policy Institute*. https://www.epi.org/publication/schools-are-still-segregated-and-black-children-are-paying-a-price/

Gay, G. (2010). *Culturally responsive teaching: Theory, research, and practice* (3rd ed.). Teachers College Press.

Gorski, P. C. (2018). *Reaching and teaching students in poverty: Strategies for erasing the opportunity gap* (2nd ed.). Teachers College Press.

Howard, G. (2016). *We can't teach what we don't know: White teachers, multiracial schools* (3rd ed.). Teachers College Press.

Joseph, R. L., & Briscoe-Smith, A. (2021). *Generation mixed goes to school: Radically listening to multiracial kids*. Teachers College Press.

Ladson-Billings, G. (2021). *Critical race theory in education: A scholar's journey*. Teachers College Press.

Lee, C. D. (2007). *Culture, literacy, and learning: Taking bloom in the midst of the whirlwind*. Teachers College Press.

Leonardo, Z. (2013). *Race frameworks: A multicultural theory of racism and education*. Teachers College Press.

Mahiri, J. (2017). *Deconstructing race: Multicultural education beyond the colorbind*. Teachers College Press.

Mayo, C. (2022). *LGBTQ youth and education: Policies and practices* (2nd ed.). Teachers College Press.

Paris, D. (2012). Culturally sustaining pedagogy: A need for change in stance, terminology, and practice. *Educational Researcher*. https://journals.sagepub.com/doi/abs/10.3102/0013189x12441244

Sensoy, O., & DiAngelo, R. (2017). *Is everyone really equal? An introduction to key concepts in social justice education* (2nd ed.). Teachers College Press.

Solórzano, D., & Huber, L. P. (2020). *Racial microaggressions: Using critical race theory in education to recognize and respond to everyday racism*. Teachers College Press.

Valdés, G. (2001). *Learning and not learning English: Latino students in American schools*. Teachers College Press.

Valdés, G., Capitelli, S., & Alvarez, L. (2011). *Latino children learning English: Steps in the journey*. Teachers College Press.

Foreword

Parents everywhere harbor a fundamental hope for their children—that they find their way to a full, happy, and independent life. The years in school are a crucial foundation for that future, especially given the global and tech-driven nature of the world they will enter. Whether or not any child is a star pupil in any given subject, the content knowledge, collaborative processes, and inquiring habits developed in the learning community of a classroom dedicated to deeper learning will serve them for a lifetime.

Unfortunately, as of this writing, the very practices that would serve our children best are under unrelenting pressure. Parental concerns are at a boiling point after 3 years of disruption to children's lives and learning, and there is little grace or patience for the time and work needed to get our schools back on track. Teachers are exhausted and beleaguered, with few reserves of strength or goodwill left after 3 years of bridging massive gaps during the pandemic. On top of it all, current political expediency has put foundational education reforms and approaches in the crosshairs of violent debate.

In the midst of the turmoil, this volume offers an essential dose of guidance and hope. Drs. Linda and Kia Darling-Hammond each bring decades of work in the field to the task of assembling the evidence base regarding the essential investments underpinning deeper learning opportunities for every one of our children. Each author has made signal contributions to our thinking about how children learn, how best to support their success, and the relationship between equity and life outcomes.

Dr. Kia Darling-Hammond's work—both her research and her experience in the field—has articulated a critical new framework for assessing health among marginalized populations, challenging us to create the conditions for children to thrive, not just survive oppression and discrimination. Here, we dig deeper to the civil rights foundation and imperative underlying real opportunities for any child to learn and thrive.

Dr. Linda Darling-Hammond has dedicated her career to advancing education research, policy, and practice that further equity and empowerment for every child. In this book, interleaved examples of research and practice help connect the dots between a civil rights foundation, classroom practice, and outcomes for students. As someone who has worked in education at all levels of practice, research, and leadership, Dr. Darling-Hammond currently serves as the president of the California State Board of Education, overseeing a long-term statewide equity strategy for the state's K–12 system. Initiated nearly a decade ago, the California strategy is a crucial test case of sustained investment under local control in order to build out supports for struggling schools, rather than taking punitive approaches.

These pages resonate with the authors' proactive commitment to high-quality educational opportunity, and the confidence that comes from intimate knowledge of the evidence base for action. These times cry out for reinvestment in our future, despite the headwinds we face. The good news is that there is clear evidence of what works, and the approaches worth fighting for. We can afford nothing less when it comes to our schools. "The path to our mutual well-being is built on equitable educational opportunity," the authors conclude. We would do well to keep pushing forward on the civil rights road to that opportunity they have so clearly laid out for us.

—Eliza Byard

Acknowledgments

We offer our heartfelt gratitude to Eliza Byard and Kent McGuire, whose partnership and passion for equity lit the spark that became this book.

In the summer of 2019, Eliza approached Kia to support a project documenting connections between civil rights conditions and educational opportunity and equity. The goal was to write a brief paper showing how important civil rights investments are to our goals for learning and to attract wide support for those investments. The U.S. presidential administration had, among other things, proposed changes to the U.S. Department of Education Civil Rights Data Collection (CRDC) that undermined its ability to track key data points (school finances, teacher experience, access to advanced coursework, etc.). Eliza had created Friends of the U.S. Commission on Civil Rights to combat efforts to undermine civil rights. Kent was a partner in the work. He was focused on highlighting the essential connection between civil rights enforcement, education equity, and deeper learning. Kia was invited to provide the research and synthesis glue.

As the paper began to expand, Kia invited Linda in as a partner, and this book took shape. It's been an exciting journey together.

We also thank our colleagues in the struggle to create equitable and empowering education for each and every child—educators, litigators, policymakers, and researchers—whose work is reflected here. We thank researchers at the Learning Policy Institute for their thought partnership on the many studies that are cited here and graphic designer Aaron Reeves for his design contributions to this project.

This research was supported by the Hewlett Foundation. The manuscript benefited from the insights and expertise of two external reviewers: John Jackson, President and CEO of the Schott Foundation for Public Education, and Gloria Ladson-Billings, Kellner Family Chair in Urban Education at the University of Wisconsin–Madison. We thank them for their care and attention to this book.

CHAPTER 1

Introduction

> Like a gardener trying to increase her fruits' growth merely by weighing them
> anew each day, we have measured and documented multiple test-score
> gaps, but we have never mounted a sustained effort to attend to the gaps in
> sustenance—in opportunities—that must be addressed before we can expect
> to see meaningful progress.
>
> —Prudence Carter and Kevin Welner, *Closing the Opportunity Gap:*
> *What America Must Do to Give Every Child an Even Chance*[1]

The nation and the world are changing rapidly. The pace seems only to accelerate each day. Knowledge is expanding, technologies are transforming every aspect of life and work, and the economy has been reshaped, as manufacturing jobs of half a century ago have been automated and outsourced. Office-based work and high-skill services combined now employ 64% of the workforce, and those workers receive 74% of overall compensation.[2] The fastest growth is in professions requiring high levels of technical, critical-thinking, and problem-solving skills[3]—skills also required to build the sustainable, equitable, and inclusive world we need. It is critical that today's students be prepared to participate meaningfully in tomorrow's diverse, global world and workforce. Consider, for example, the needs of our aging populace, which depends on younger generations for Social Security investment, caregiving, and their capacity to exert compassion and wisdom in the design and maintenance of our larger social, economic, and political infrastructures.

Our young people need education that prepares them to engage in a global, technologically mediated future. Thus, *deeper learning*—once allocated to the small share of students presumed to be preparing for "thinking work" requiring higher-order knowledge and skills—should be available to all. As described by the Hewlett Foundation, deeper learning offers "the skills and knowledge that students must possess to succeed in 21st-century jobs and civic life."[4] These include six competencies: (1) mastering core academic content, (2) thinking critically and solving complex problems, (3) communicating effectively, (4) working collaboratively, (5) learning how to learn, and (6) developing academic mindsets.[5] In other words, young people need to be prepared to engage intellectually, in addition to developing interpersonal and technical skills.

Furthermore, as the world and nation have grappled with the COVID-19 pandemic, concerns about losing jobs to automation have been met with calls for acknowledging the attributes that machines cannot exhibit: the human capacity for *social cognition*, including "judgment, empathy, intuition, creativity, ethics, curiosity, and comprehension of complex interactions among . . . humans."[6] A knowledgeable, thoughtful, caring public is essential for a democratic society.

Yet the journey to deeper learning possibilities is a challenging one in the inequitable school system we have inherited in the United States. Not only was a "thinking curriculum" that engaged students in deeper learning once reserved for the small number of students selected for gifted and talented programs and advanced courses, but historically, it also has been available more often in affluent schools in predominantly White communities and has been considered unnecessary or inappropriate for students of color and those from low-income communities.[7] Compounding these presumptions about who is entitled to a deeper learning curriculum are the many other sources of inequality in our society that make it difficult for many schools to offer, and many young people to profit from, such learning opportunities.

Equity requires a policy system that provides every student with access to an education focused on meaningful learning, taught by competent and caring educators who have the knowledge and skills to teach diverse learners effectively, and supported by adequate resources that provide the conditions for effective learning.[8] And young people need contexts that support their safety and health so they can participate in school successfully. They must have access to supportive learning conditions and opportunities, so schools need not only to be well resourced but also inclusive and organized to provide skillful teaching, affirmation, and innovative, high-quality curricula (see Figure 1.1).

Such access is not a given. In fact, it has long been a point of struggle. For centuries, access to a free and equal education has required the continuous articulation and enforcement of rights, and our campaign is still ongoing. The inequalities in our society are so deep-seated that clearing a path to deeper learning for marginalized young people has required—and continues to require—considerable engagement in civil rights litigation, enforcement, and advocacy. While civil rights enforcement cannot by itself ensure deeper learning, it forms a crucial foundation by holding actors in our vast systems of schooling accountable for equity and inclusion. In order to benefit from innovative practices, children need conditions that make rich learning possible. Schools that prioritize children's *right to learn* are more likely to adopt policies and practices conducive to deeper learning.

In this book, we describe key civil conditions and actions essential to paving a way toward deeper learning. The work begins and ends with access—to safety, support, opportunity, and a future full of possibility.

DEEPER LEARNING IN ACTION

To understand what we are working toward, we take a look at deeper learning in practice in two distinctive sites: an elementary school in New York City and

Figure 1.1. The Civil Rights Road to Deeper Learning

a secondary school in California. Both schools have worked to create contexts for supportive, empowering learning for students who would have been left out and left behind were it not for civil rights advances over many decades and innovative educators who could build on those foundations.

MIDTOWN WEST ELEMENTARY SCHOOL

In Ted Pollen's 4th-grade classroom at Midtown West school in New York City, a group of 27 racially, ethnically, and linguistically diverse students is deeply engaged in a mathematics inquiry focused on understanding the concepts of range, mean, median, and mode. Some are seated around tables, while others are in pairs or trios on the rug in the classroom meeting area. While some teachers might introduce the four terms with definitions and rules for calculating them and give students a worksheet of problems to fill out, Ted's class has been conducting a study that provided them with the data they are now analyzing. Earlier in the week, they measured and recorded the height of everyone in their own classroom and all the children in one of the kindergarten classrooms who are their reading buddies. Each then figured out how to display the data distributions with bar graphs they constructed individually, so as to be able to figure out the range, mean, median, and mode for each class and compare them. Working in teams, they use various tools, such as manipulatives and calculators, as they advise and query one another about what to do.

Ted—a graduate of and now mentor teacher for Bank Street College—and his two student teachers move unobtrusively among groups, watching the process and occasionally asking questions to help move students to the next level of understanding. It's clear that he is thinking about students' zones of proximal development as he chooses his questions. Ted says to one group: "Think about your design. What's the best way of displaying the data so you can make an actual comparison?" In another, he asks, "Can someone give me the range for kindergarten? Our range? Are there any outliers?" This led to a realization that there was little overlap between the two groups, but there were a few relatively short 4th graders and one very tall kindergartner. A student said proudly, pointing to that data point: "That's my reading buddy!"

In yet another group Ted observes to one of the boys, "You're having the same problem that she's having," pointing to a tablemate to encourage the two of them to work together. They begin counting and calculating to solve the problem jointly. Ted never gives away the answer, but he assists the problem-solving process with questions that carefully scaffold student understanding. In their groups, students engage in vigorous debates about the answers, explaining their reasoning to one another, re-counting their data, marshalling evidence, and demonstrating their solutions in different ways. Ted does not attempt to adjudicate the disputes or provide the right answer. He allows the groups to work through the problem.

Ted watches over an autistic student working with a one-on-one aide. The student sings to herself periodically while she progresses through her work. In the hubbub of the classroom, her singing is not a distraction to the others, as they all focus intently on communicating to find solutions to this highly motivating puzzle. Every single student has made significant progress in developing a deep understanding of these key statistical concepts that often elude students much older than themselves.

After about 45 minutes of in-depth mathematics work, Ted asks the students to "keep all of your data together in your math folder" to come back to tomorrow. As everyone cleans up their work and puts their folder away, Ted quietly sings an African song while he sets up snack. Students come in groups to receive their crackers and go back to their seats. Ted's singing shifts to English: "In everything we do and everything we say, you and I are making history today." This signals to students that what they do matters and is important. It is also a reminder of the historical references Ted has placed all around them.

Around the hard-working groups of children, student work covers the walls. A classroom constitution that was collectively developed and signed by each student and teacher is displayed, along with a "Problem Parking Lot" with sticky notes listing problems and questions the class has agreed to return to. Handmade globes and a timeline string with chronological date cards of important events hang from the ceiling. The meeting area in front of a whiteboard is covered with a rug that is a map of the world.

Especially prominent are student accounts of the lives of enslaved people in New Amsterdam and New York, 1621–1680, along with posters illustrating various fractions problems they have tackled and solved, including how they have split sub sandwiches among various odd numbers of people. On the back shelves, one set of tubs offers manipulatives for mathematics. Another set of tubs includes books labeled by type, all connected to current topics of study: Authors who have been studied by the class each merit a tub, as do African-American Biographies, Slavery, Other Biographies, Ted's Favorites, and more.

Also on the wall are many posters reminding students about their routines. One summarizes the rules for Book Club. Another asks, "What is figurative language?," clarifying that it is "when words mean something other than their literal meaning." The poster defines what most would think of as high school terms: simile, metaphor, hyperbole, personification, alliteration, onomatopoeia, idiom, allusion, and oxymoron, offering concrete examples of each.

Other posters developed by students and teacher include a "Writing workshop conferencing protocol," "Poetry guidelines," "Persuasive essays," "Jobs in a reading conference" (enumerated for both the student and the teacher), and "Elements of a news magazine article." These are often in the students' own words, codifying their learning so they can share it and go back to it as needed. Another poster enumerates "What we know about maps," while still another describes "Multiplying 2-digit by 1-digit numbers: The traditional algorithm."

Invisible in this moment are the school supports that make this productive hubbub possible: Free breakfasts for all children; free transportation for children who live in temporary housing; a Family Center that offers educational workshops, cultural connections, and family support services; extended after-school time and services; and twice-annual student–family–teacher conferences. The school also commits itself to a set of children's rights that include "I have a right to be happy and to be treated with compassion in this school"; "I have a right to be myself in this school. This means that no one will treat me unfairly"; and "I have the right to be safe in this school." Community-building and conflict resolution are explicit, schoolwide efforts. Although the school is overcrowded, it is welcoming in every respect.

Source: Adapted from Darling-Hammond, L., & Oakes, J., with Wojcikiewicz, S. K., Hyler, M. E., Guha, R., Podolsky, A., Kini, T., Cook-Harvey, C. M., Mercer, C. J., & Harrell, A. (2019). *Preparing teachers for deeper learning.* Harvard Education Press.

This short vignette illustrates how Midtown West and Ted Pollen's class are grounded in a developmental framework that leverages strong and trusting relationships, collaboration in the learning process, connections to prior experience, teaching that promotes inquiry undergirded by explicit instruction, and support for both individualized and collective learning.

Authentic, engaging tasks with real-world connections motivate student effort and engagement, which is supported through teacher scaffolding and a wide range of tools that allow for personalized learning and student agency. Other scaffolds—like the charts reminding students of their learning processes and key concepts—support self-regulation and strategic learning while reducing cognitive load, in order to facilitate higher-order thinking and performance skills. These also enable student self-assessment, as well as peer and teacher feedback that are part of an ongoing formative assessment process. Routines for reflection on and revision of work support the development of metacognition and a growth mindset. Meanwhile, students' identities as competent writers, scientists, and mathematicians are also reinforced, as their own work dominates the walls of the classroom and is the focus of the learning process.

All students feel they belong in this room, where they are learning to become responsible community members, critical thinkers, and problem-solvers together. That sense of inclusion is buoyed by both a range of culturally connected curriculum units and materials and a wide array of school supports that address student and family needs while including them as partners in the educational process.

SAN FRANCISCO INTERNATIONAL HIGH SCHOOL

Across the country from Midtown West Elementary School, a 9th- and 10th-grade biology class at San Francisco International High School (SFIHS) focuses on a central question: "Should soda have a tax?" The group of 25 students, roughly divided between 9th- and 10th-graders, includes several students who have been in the United States for 6 months or less. In this high school designed for newcomers, even the class veterans have been in the United States for less than two years.

SFIHS is one of 30 U.S. schools in the Internationals Network for Public Schools, an organization that designs and runs public school programs for refugee and immigrant multilingual learners in collaboration with school districts across the county.

As in other project-based learning environments, instruction for this heterogeneous class connects learning principles (here, in biology) to real-world issues (nutrition and policy). The veteran teacher, Patricia, has built into her lesson extensive scaffolds designed to meet students at their English language acquisition, content knowledge, and skill development levels. She moves through the classroom engaging individual students, small groups of students, and the whole class.

She intentionally leverages the assets that her students have brought to the classroom, particularly their native language fluency. The core question is written in English and the five other languages spoken by students in the class to give them an immediate starting point for engaging with the content questions. She also employs other techniques that allow students to use their native languages to support themselves and one another in engaging with the rigorous content. For example, throughout the classroom, students use Google Translate to translate words from Spanish, Arabic, and other languages. In contrast to classrooms in which students' native languages are minimized or seen through a deficit lens, students leverage their home languages to make meaning of complex grade-level academic content. With students from multiple linguistic backgrounds, English is the common language and the language of formal academic discourse, yet English is not positioned as the only valuable language. The assets-based classroom environment makes students comfortable taking risks to speak, read, and write in English, but they also use their native languages as a valuable tool to be harnessed and developed.

Patricia also takes steps to make instruction and content accessible and to further students' vocabulary and writing development. For example, she prominently displays visuals from earlier lessons that students have labeled, and she has research articles and documents readily available so that students can access them throughout the inquiry process. In addition, each portion of the lesson is carefully chunked into discrete sections to allow students to understand the content and to apply their emerging English skills. For instance, students examine pictures relevant to the soda tax debate and connect those pictures with academic English words they have learned in previous lessons (e.g., "glucose"). One chunked exercise includes the following stages:

Each student chooses one picture and labels it in English with scientific terms that have previously been taught.

In small groups, students discuss the pictures using English:

- What did other people write?
- What did it make you think?

Next, using the labeled pictures from their groups, students individually write "a complex sentence" in English that can be used in their final essays. In doing so, students need to use the English words "but," "because," or "so," e.g., "When you don't eat, the glucose decreases because your body uses the energy."

During the lesson, the teacher moves throughout the room meeting individually with students to make sure can successfully engage with the language and content. She also draws on the board, points to visual scaffolds arrayed on the walls, and gestures as if playing charades, all to make her meaning clearer. She has developed a series of sounds that the students associate with an action (e.g., an action that encourages students to look at their peers who are speaking or an action that encourages students to use sentence starters that are on the walls). This simple yet effective method for providing reminders and tools seems to help ease the cognitive load for her students, who are doing far more than the typical native English speaker would be doing in such a class. She repeatedly reminds her students of her expectations for participation and reinforces participation and structural routines to keep students engaged.

Eventually, students build from these smaller tasks to craft thesis statements and ultimately write persuasive essays in English that support their position on the value of soda taxes. While the development of academic English related to the content is clearly scaffolded through these steps, Patricia also focuses on science, engaging the students on both the biology and chemistry around sugary drinks' effect on humans and the social science behind their impact on communities. Over the course of multiple weeks, students develop the content knowledge and the English literacy skills needed to engage orally and in writing on the topic in sophisticated ways.

This instructional approach does not occur by happenstance; it is an intentional approach supported by a web of mutually reinforcing school design features.

For instance, the Internationals Network deliberately uses mixed-age, heterogeneous classes to support students' language, academic, and sociocultural development. Mixed-age grouping, which pairs 9th- and 10th-graders or 11th- and 12th-graders, recognizes that students are multidimensional and are not at the same level for all areas of knowledge, including life experience, content knowledge, and different language modalities. In addition, this heterogeneous structure allows students with more developed language and academic skills to support novice peers. This practice is particularly valuable for new students who are recent arrivals to the United States. In the 9th- and 10th-grade class described earlier, two 9th-graders had arrived in the United States and at the school just a few days before that observation. The teacher had intentionally grouped those students with 10th-graders who spoke their native languages (in this case, Spanish and Arabic) and who could act as mentors and provide academic, language, sociocultural, and emotional support to the newcomers.

In the 9th and 10th grades, these mixed-age classes also loop, or stay with the same set of interdisciplinary teachers, for 2 years, enabling the development of strong relationships between students and teachers. This continuity also generates academic benefits, as teachers can use their knowledge of students' strengths and struggles to meet their academic and linguistic needs over a longer period of time. Each student is also part of an advisory group that loops for 2 years, meeting several times a week; the advisor is the point person and advocate for the student and family, operating advisory classes that provide a family environment for academic, social, and emotional learning and support. Overall, the structures of mixed-age grouping and looping allow Internationals to support students in deeper learning while scaffolding their academic and linguistic development.

In addition to advisories, SFIHS provides extensive supports for students. Internationals have dedicated staff (e.g., social workers, counselors) who work closely with teachers and students to provide academic and social-emotional supports. School staff also provide access to services and programs as part of typical day-to-day school operations. For instance, schools have devised age-appropriate approaches to providing students with meals so that little public attention is called to their needs. At SFIHS, there are before- and after-school clubs where full meals are included, as a significant number of students eat all of their meals at school. The schools also have strategies to address a number of other issues that immigrant youth face, including tackling mental health challenges, providing education and support regarding immigration rights, and offering assistance to access food stamps, health care, and other social services; housing; part-time employment; and college. Taken together, each of the design features articulated above combine to create a strong web of support so students can learn and grow.

Source: Adapted from Roc, M., Ross, P., & Hernández, L. E. (2019). *Internationals Network for Public Schools: A deeper learning approach to supporting English learners* (pp. 1–2, 11–12, 23). Learning Policy Institute.

THE CIVIL RIGHTS FOUNDATION

Deeper learning opportunities at Midtown West in New York City and San Francisco International High School are possible both because of the thoughtful, committed educators who designed and operate the schools and because of the many civil rights advocates who have made access to such schools possible for young people who would otherwise be excluded.

From the time Southern states made it illegal to teach enslaved people to read, through the 19th century and into the 20th, racially and ethnically minoritized students have faced de facto and de jure exclusion from public schools throughout the nation. As the United States stood poised to end the institution of slavery in the mid-1800s, and during the decades afterward, numerous cases and efforts laid the groundwork for the educational equity fight we still face—a fight needed to offer well-funded, -staffed, and -resourced schools with high-quality, holistic supports to students of color and language-minority students.

To trace just some of that fight, it is important to recall that while Southern states made it a crime to teach an enslaved person to read, discrimination in the provision of education was also occurring in the North. In 1857, for example, a group of Black leaders protested to a New York State investigating committee that the New York board of education spent $16 per White child and only one cent per Black child for school buildings. While Black students occupied schools described as "dark and cheerless" in neighborhoods "full of vice and filth," White students had access to buildings that were "splendid, almost palatial edifices, with manifold comforts, conveniences, and elegancies."[9]

Several years earlier, in *Roberts v. City of Boston* (1849), the Massachusetts Supreme Court had ruled segregated schools constitutional in that state. This set precedent for the federal 1896 *Plessy v. Ferguson* decision a half-century later, which ruled that Louisiana's "separate but equal" law was constitutional. This, in turn, opened the way for the cascade of Jim Crow laws that then took hold and launched what we now know as the segregation era—an era riddled with battles between those dedicated to freedom and those committed to maintaining an unequal status quo.

In the years between *Roberts* and *Plessy*, the nation saw the 1857 *Dred Scott* decision denying citizenship to Black people, the Civil War, and emancipation of enslaved people in the District of Columbia, followed by a federal emancipation proclamation, passage of the Thirteenth through Fifteenth Amendments, the Civil Rights Act of 1866 guaranteeing equal rights under the law, the Civil Rights Act of 1875 banning racial discrimination in public accommodations (undermined in 1883), several enforcement acts intended to ensure compliance with new protective laws, and, in the tug of war between opportunity and oppression, the advent of Jim Crow laws.

These battles over rights and protections continued amidst two world wars. Litigation seeking access to schools on the part of American Indians,[10] Mexican Americans, and Black Americans were all part of the suite of actions that informed *Brown v. Board of Education* in 1954. One such historic case was *Mendez v. Westminster* (1946), a class action suit brought by over 5,000 Mexican American students in California, which posed the first successful constitutional challenge to *Plessy*.[11] Underneath every inch forward and against every setback could be found the painstaking labor of brave individuals, abolitionists, and allies—including children and youth.

More than a decade after the Supreme Court had already declared "separate but equal" education to be a violation of the 14th Amendment, James Bryant Conant's *Slums and Suburbs* documented continuing disparities in educational opportunity, including spending in suburban districts that was twice that of segregated inner-city schools. These disparities, although somewhat reduced in the 1960s and 1970s during the civil rights movement and the War on Poverty, have returned in full force and characterize U.S. education for many students today, just as they did more than 50 years ago. This is especially true for the children of those who did not squeak through the door of opportunity when it opened a crack in the late 1960s, before it slammed shut again in the 1980s as equity policies were removed during the Reagan administration.

These inequities are in part a function of how public education in the United States is funded. In most cases, education costs are supported primarily by local property taxes, along with state grants-in-aid that are typically insufficient to close the gaps caused by differences in local property values. Rich districts can spend more, even when poorer districts tax themselves at proportionally higher rates. Even within districts, schools serving more advantaged students have often had more access to the resources for learning—funding, well-qualified educators, quality curriculum, and specialized supports—than those serving students of color, new immigrants, and children from low-income households. The battle for equitable educational access has been fought on all these fronts and continues today.

Every advance has brought benefits both to individuals who access greater opportunity and to society as a whole. For example, desegregation results in overall academic gains for students, in part because low-poverty, predominantly White schools are typically better resourced than segregated schools serving students of color. This phenomenon likely explains, at least partially, why the Black students in Rucker Johnson's national longitudinal study of desegregation, *Children of the Dream,* saw better long-term outcomes: The desegregated schools they were able to attend under court orders were better funded, with smaller class sizes and less staff turnover.[12] For this and other reasons—including smaller classes, a robust curriculum, and a range of out-of-classroom supports—students of color in racially diverse schools experienced a boost to their academic performance,[13] including higher graduation rates[14] and stronger wages, less poverty, and lower rates of incarceration as adults.[15] All of these outcomes bring benefits to society, as better education helps graduates participate more fully in the economy, generating greater tax revenue to support schools, health care, and social services.

Every advance, however, has not been perfect, as desegregation also caused the displacement of talented, well-trained, caring Black educators and administrators whose commitment to their students was irreplaceable.[16] A well-resourced school can only be responsive to the holistic needs of students of color when its adult personnel understand, support, and respect students' and families' inherent dignity. Research[17] has demonstrated time and again how important representation is for students with minoritized social identities; the work to populate schools with increasingly representative teachers, staff, and administrators continues.

In the space of education, in particular, civil rights enforcement has been an essential strategy for the improvement of all students' opportunities to learn and contribute to society. Such efforts have been beneficial not only to targeted populations but to larger communities as well. For example, schools that build a positive climate using social and emotional learning, rather than zero-tolerance discipline, see academic performance benefits for *all* student groups.[18] Students educated in diverse, well-funded schools can experience greater comfort with and understanding of the perspectives of people different from them, in addition to developing strong civic engagement and improved critical thinking, communication, and problem-solving.[19] Furthermore, desegregation in schools can support desegregation of communities, as people who have "early and sustained" exposure are more likely to choose similarly diverse environments when they're older.[20]

In a 2011 conversation with the Center for American Progress, Tom Perez, then Assistant Attorney General for the Civil Rights Division at the U.S. Department of Justice, said that his job was "to build an opportunity society," characterized by "the opportunity to learn through the enforcement of education laws, to earn through the enforcement of employment laws, to realize the American dream through the enforcement of fair housing and fair lending laws, and to be safe through police misconduct reform."[21] Beyond basic access, opportunity and safety are key organizing principles for the right to learn, and they influence the extent to which young people can engage in deeper learning that actualizes their dreams, passions, and potential. Because access to a genuine right to learn is linked to housing quality, neighborhood investment, environmental conditions, public spaces, economic realities, and enfranchisement, making progress on civil rights agendas like these also supports education.

In addition to the hard-won gains of litigation, the federal government and states have moved civil rights forward through guidance (e.g., Obama-era guidance on district approaches to school integration)[22] and strategic investment (e.g. funding for interdistrict desegregation strategies like those launched in Connecticut, Massachusetts, and Nebraska).[23] In this book, we speak not only to the importance of access to a safe environment and equitably funded schools (in Chapters 2 and 3), but also to the power of robust state and district-level investments in wraparound services and restorative practices that enable students to learn and be well (Chapter 4); policies needed to recruit, support, and retain a representative and stable body of well-qualified educators who know how to support diverse learners engaged in meaningful learning in all schools (Chapter 5); and access to a high-quality, whole- child–centered, deeper learning curriculum (Chapter 6). In Chapter 7, we summarize the steps needed to move forward on the civil rights road to deeper learning.

CHAPTER 2

A Safe and Healthy Community

The laws that codify racial segregation have been eradicated but the practices continue today, which is why you get refineries, chemical plants and landfills disproportionately in communities of color. There have been four decades of studies documenting that it's not land values or property values—the most potent variable is race. It's the driver of who gets pollution and who doesn't.[1]

—Robert Bullard

To understand children's school experiences and outcomes, we have to begin *outside* of schools—in the neighborhoods and communities where young people live. Both beyond and within schools, children's developmental needs must be supported if children are to have access to academic success. It is also in these spaces that we see critical civil rights engagement—around such issues as technology equity,[2] economic opportunity,[3] pollution, and fair housing—all of which carry developmental and educational implications. At the foundation of the civil rights road to deeper learning is a safe and healthy community.

Under our current educational system, so-called "achievement gaps" for disadvantaged children begin early—even before they enter school—and widen over time.[4] This is a function of significant *opportunity* gaps in multiple areas of these children's lives.[5] Citing the U.S. General Accounting Office, the Centers for Disease Control and Prevention (CDC), and numerous scholars, Richard Rothstein's *The Color of Law* lists such contributing factors as low access to eyeglasses; disproportionate instances of lead poisoning, iron-deficiency anemia, and asthma, compounded by substandard pediatric care; housing instability; neighborhood dangers; and fewer opportunities for extracurricular enrichments (which might require extra funds or transportation).[6]

The U.S. Department of Education reported in 2013 that 22% of America's K–12 students lived in conditions of poverty.[7] Nearly half of the student population qualified for free or reduced-price lunches, and poverty rates were disproportionately high for students of color.[8] Despite a gradual decline in rates prior to the pandemic, these numbers shifted for the worse between 2019 and 2020, with a reversal of progress, increases for communities of color, and a widening of the gap by race/ethnicity and family structure. As Child Trends reported in 2021:

Poverty rates among Latino children rose by 4.2 percentage points, from 23.0 percent to 27.3 percent, and by 2.8 percentage points among Black children, from 26.4 percent to 29.2 percent. . . . In contrast, the rates of White and Asian children in poverty remained relatively stable. In addition, children in female-headed families also saw a large increase in the poverty rate, by 4.1 percentage points, from 33.4 percent to 37.4 percent.[9]

Having fewer resources has meant lack of access to learning technologies (computers, stable and reliable Internet connections) that became especially critical during the pandemic. It has also meant growing rates of homelessness, compounded by high rates of unemployment that also frequently mean lack of health care. Equitable education requires multi-systemic solutions—through economic, political, social service, and health care reforms, which, in turn, requires a holistic approach to resourcing communities as well as schools so that children are able to begin life with the fundamentals on which their learning depends.

One of the most egregious aspects of environmental inequity is that people of color, particularly Native, Black, and Latinx communities, are disproportionately exposed to toxins and stressors. Manuel Pastor and Rachel Morello-Frosch describe this as "environmental inequality—the tendency for environmental disamenities to be disproportionately located in low-income communities of color."[10] They note that this "pattern of environmental disparity seems more pronounced by race than by income, a trend that suggests that inequalities are not merely a function of market forces or of wealth, but also are due to structural racism and its interaction with power over, for example, permitting decisions and the siting of toxic facilities."[11]

The issue interacts with schooling and learning as well. A 2004 study of exposure to ambient air toxicity and estimated respiratory and cancer risks among Los Angeles Unified School District students found that:

schools proximate to [Toxic Release Inventory] facilities . . . exhibit a 16% gap from those not proximate . . . whereas schools located in tracts with the highest estimated respiratory hazard have a performance differential of about 20% compared with schools located in tracts with the lowest risk level. This 20% differential [roughly matches] the average difference between the bottom third and middle third of schools in terms of academic performance.[12]

Cleaning up the air would "yield an estimated performance boost of over 10%."[13] The researchers' calculations related to an "environmental effect" explained one third of the poverty variable and one tenth, overall, of the roughly 20% academic performance gap between White and Black students in the district.[14] These results control for both socioeconomic and demographic factors.

The authors note that "lifetime cancer risk associated with cumulative exposure to ambient air toxics [sic] [is] unequal by race—even when [accounting] for income, local land use, and other factors generally deemed relevant to local air-pollution levels."[15] Such exposure carries a public health cost, which diminishes human and economic capacity. The results are recursive: People become ill and suffer numerous challenges to daily living; this in turn increases stress, as well as exposure to substandard care, which in turn keeps people ill.[16] From a schooling standpoint, educators seeking to support increased opportunity for children have to contend with these external, chronic, and life-truncating factors, which are widespread across the country. As an Earthjustice report notes:

> For more than five years there has been a water crisis in Flint, Michigan. Meanwhile, in White Hall, Alabama, residents live with raw sewage because basic sanitation is not affordable. The fifth district of Saint James Parish in Louisiana is known as "Cancer Alley." The concentration of industrial petrochemical plants causes high rates of cancer among local residents there. All of these cases are in predominantly Black areas. Studies show that Black people are 75% more likely to live near oil and gas refineries, and Black Americans face higher risks of premature death from power plant pollution.[17]

ENVIRONMENTAL INJUSTICE AND EDUCATION: THE CASE OF FLINT, MICHIGAN

A vivid contemporary example of the quantifiable impact of environmental inequity is the mass lead poisoning of the children of Flint, MI, and the larger community—particularly in the wards with the highest concentrations of poverty. Over 70% of the children impacted are Black. The civil rights dimensions of the case are significant, relating to environmental racism, school policy and infrastructure, disenfranchisement, and housing.

By the time its lead poisoning crisis began, Flint had suffered decades of hardship brought on by racist disinvestment, poverty, violence, and depopulation. As one analysis noted, "About 43% of the population lived in poverty, 45% of homes were renter-occupied, only 11% of the population had a bachelor's degree or higher, and almost 13% of persons younger than 65 years were without health insurance."[18]

In 2012, Flint residents were stripped of their ability to elect local representatives when the city's debt was used to justify the imposition of state control and a state-appointed emergency manager. By April 2014, this decision resulted in a choice to switch the city's water supply from Lake Huron, which was treated by the Detroit Water and Sewerage Department, to the Flint River water source, which was not properly treated.[19] The result was contamination that exposed over 100,000 people, including nearly 30,000 children, to lead in the water, as well as two outbreaks of Legionnaires' disease (between 2014 and 2015) that killed 12 people and sickened more than 80 in Flint and Genesee County.

Residents' complaints about the change in water quality—evident in its color, smell, and taste—were ignored, even as more of them developed rashes, hair loss, and illness. It took until August 2014 for the city of Flint to issue a water boiling advisory and boost chlorine levels after detecting bacteria. In January 2015, Flint issued another water advisory, this time due to detection of concentrations of carcinogenic disinfecting by-products. That same month, the University of Michigan–Flint revealed that testing had found elevated lead levels in its water.[20] A blog post published by the American Civil Liberties Union's (ACLU) Michigan branch on June 25, 2015—more than a year past the water source change—stated:

> Perhaps no Michigan city best exemplifies our worsening water woes more than Flint, the once-thriving auto manufacturing town whose emergency manager severed the city's ties to the Detroit water and sewerage system and ordered that water from the Flint River be pumped into local homes and businesses. Since then, water bills have continued to rise. Residents have complained that the water is not only smelly and brown, but has left some residents physically ill. Yet, despite their cries, city leaders insist that everything is alright.[21]

The city of Flint would not issue a lead advisory until September 25, 2015, after pediatrician Mona Hanna-Attisha reported finding high levels of lead in the blood of children ages 5 and younger, and later, scientists from Virginia Tech University tested the water. Just over a week prior to the advisory, the Michigan Department of Environmental Quality had asserted that the city's water was safe. Two weeks after the Genesee County Health Department declared a public health emergency on October 1, 2015, Flint was reconnected to Great Lakes water. The severely corroded pipes and plumbing, however, continued to leach lead into the drinking water and terrible damage had already been done.[22]

In January 2016, the American Civil Liberties Union (ACLU) of Michigan, the Natural Resources Defense Council (NRDC), a Flint resident, and the group Concerned Pastors for Social Action filed suit. On March 21, 2016, the governor-commissioned Flint Water Advisory Task Force concluded that the Michigan Department of Environmental Quality bore "primary responsibility for the water contamination in Flint [and] caused [the] crisis to happen."[23] Although a judge ruled later that year that the state and city were responsible for providing clean water (bottled delivery) to residents, both entities refused to comply. A settlement was reached in 2017 requiring a state-subsidized replacement of the city's lead and galvanized steel water lines by 2020.

The educational costs of these civil rights violations have been and continue to be enormous. It's important to begin with an understanding that there is no safe level of lead exposure for humans. In children, exposure can lead to "damage to the brain and nervous system; slowed growth and development; learning and behavior problems; and hearing and speech problems. . . . In adults, [it] can increase risk for high blood pressure, heart disease, kidney disease, and reduced fertility."[24] Lead exposure is also implicated in reduced birth weight and increased fetal deaths, while the resulting changes in DNA methylation can be passed down epigenetically across multiple generations.[25] In Flint, elevated blood lead levels were measured at dangerous thresholds, with notable increases for both children and adults after the switch in water supply.[26]

Lead Poisoning and Educational Outcomes

An April 2015 report published by the CDC offers a summary of research into the educational impact of lead exposure (see Table 2.1).

The CDC report goes on to detail the neurodevelopmental consequences of lead exposure, populations at risk, implications for educational attainment, risk-reduction programs, and corrective response programs and federal policies, and provides guidance on how to obtain services in the event of lead poisoning and resulting disability.[27]

Even as efforts to address the infrastructural and environmental crisis were underway, requests for related special education, behavioral intervention, and care in schools began almost immediately and continued to rise. *New York Times* journalist Erica L. Green reported this account about one local educator:

> Bethany Dumanois, who has taught in Flint for 25 years, works two jobs to keep teaching because she said she cannot abandon children whose discolored, rash-covered skin and chunks of exposed scalp haunt her. In the earlier days of the crisis, she spent class time addressing questions from her students about whether they would die from the water like their class lizard, a bearded dragon, did.[28]

Litigation for Educational Redress

Flint's public school district was already struggling under the weight of a sizable budget deficit ($21 million), resulting in staffing cuts and the lowest teacher compensation rates in its county. It was a system already in distress. In violation of federal law, special education students were being segregated from their peers during the school day, with insufficient personnel available to meet students' needs. The Flint special education student dropout rate in 2013–2014 was nearly double the statewide average (15.5% vs. 8.63%), and the following school year saw 13% of special education students suspended or expelled for more than 10 days (more than five times the statewide rate).[29]

A class-action lawsuit (*D.R. v. Michigan Department of Education*) brought by the ACLU of Michigan, the Education Law Center, and the New York–based firm of White & Case on October 18, 2016, claimed that the Michigan Department of Education, the Genesee Intermediate School District, and Flint Community Schools were in violation of state and federal laws (including the Individuals With Disabilities Education Act) by both failing to provide students with sufficient special education identification and support and then punishing children for disability-related behavior through restraints, suspension, expulsion, and arrest, a situation exacerbated by the lead exposure.

The suit made possible the opening of the $3 million Neurodevelopmental Center of Excellence in 2018. There, targeted, comprehensive neuropsychological

Table 2.1. Research on the Impact of Lead Exposure on Children

Blood Lead Levels (µg/dL)	Educational Impact	Size of Study (# of children)	Study Location
≤ 3 µg/dL	Decreased end of grade test scores	More than 57,000 children	North Carolina
4 µg/dL at three years of age	Increased likelihood of learning disabled classification in elementary school	More than 57,000 children	North Carolina
	Poorer performance on tests	35,000 children	Connecticut
5 µg/dL	30% more likely to fail 3rd-grade reading and math tests	More than 48,000 children	Chicago, IL
	More likely to be non-proficient in math, science, and reading	21,000 children	Detroit, MI
5–9 µg/dL	Scored 4.5 points lower on reading readiness tests	3,406 children	Rhode Island
≥ 10 µg/dL	Scored 10.1 points lower on reading readiness tests	3,406 children	Rhode Island
10–19 µg/dL	Significantly lower academic performance test scores in 4th grade	More than 3,000 children	Milwaukee, WI
≥ 25 µg/dL	$0.5 million in excess annual special education and juvenile justice costs	279 children	Mahoning County, OH

Source: Adapted from Educational Services for Children Affected by Lead Expert Panel. (2015). *Educational interventions for children affected by lead.* U.S. Department of Health and Human Services, p. viii. https://www.cdc.gov/nceh/lead/publications/educational_interventions_children_affected_by_lead.pdf

screening for all children who had been exposed to lead confirmed the presence of a range of disabilities. Green writes, "[In 2018–19], when one in five students qualified for special education services, one in every four special education teaching positions was unfilled."[30] By the 2019–2020 school year, the percentage of Flint students who qualified for special education services had risen to 28%, nearly double what it had been at the start of the lead exposure crisis, and 70% of the students evaluated by the city's screening center had required accommodations for challenges like ADHD, dyslexia, or mild intellectual impairment.[31] Additional investments in special education services and preschool have followed from the state and the county as part of a settlement of the ACLU lawsuit, while a variety of other lawsuits have continued against a wide range of defendants.[32]

As processes of accountability and repair were beginning to unfold 4 years into the crisis, ACLU investigative reporter Curt Guyette offered two poignant observations: that "the law—which the governor's own task force acknowledged led to this nightmare—still [hadn't] been repealed, or even altered at all" and that "when everything's accounted for, the emergency manager's decision to save $5 million could easily end up costing taxpayers well over $1 billion."[33] More importantly, it has exposed thousands of children to disability and difficulty in a system ill-equipped to meet their needs. The crisis reveals the shortcomings of an education policy system whose only answer in 2014 to these harms to children's learning was the punitive accountability system offered by No Child Left Behind that blamed the education system for low performance and sought to remediate low test scores by firing teachers and closing public schools.[34]

BEYOND FLINT

Lead poisoning is not a new concern in the United States. The government began banning lead in gasoline in 1972 and in paint in 1978; however, people still live in buildings that contain lead paint, lead has leached into the soil from years of car emissions and industry, and lead pipes are still in use in cities across the nation. The U.S. Environmental Protection Agency (EPA) has estimated there are 7.3 million lead service lines nationwide, servicing as many as 10 million homes, and replacing them would strain municipal resources.[35] According to the CDC, roughly 24 million homes in the nation contain deteriorating lead paint, and 4 million of them house small children. Between the paint, the soil, and the water, marginalized communities experience systemic exposure.[36] Nelson reported that between 2007 and 2010, about 6% of Black children and 2% of White children were found to have lead blood levels of at least 5 micrograms per deciliter, nationally.[37] Furthermore, numerous cities throughout the country have higher rates of pediatric lead exposure than Flint, including Detroit, Milwaukee, and Cleveland.[38] Unlike Flint, these cities have not been subject to the public attention and litigation that could correct the violations of health and learning that their children experience.

A study released in January 2019 by the Harvard School of Public Health and the University of California Agriculture and Natural Resources Nutrition Policy Institute found not only that half the nation's students attend schools in states that have no programs testing for lead in drinking water, but that in states that do, roughly 40% of the samples have revealed elevated lead levels.[39] Investigative journalist Corey Mitchell reported in 2019 that the EPA "estimates that 98,000 public schools and a half-million child-care facilities are not regulated under the Safe Drinking Water Act, the federal law designed to ensure safe drinking water. In fact, there is no federal policy that mandates lead testing in schools."[40] Lead exposure poses a lifelong developmental threat and an intergenerational epigenetic threat that disproportionately affects economically underresourced communities—communities that are disproportionately people of color. The finding in Flint that the crisis had roots in historical and ongoing policy and practice is applicable nationally, pointing to the need for further civil rights action around environmental and housing policy.

Redlining and Environmental Threat

Redlining is a practice that was born when the Home Owners Loan Corporation created color-coded maps rating perceived investment risk in the 1930s. It left Black neighborhoods coded red to indicate they were too risky to receive the economic revitalization (including Federal Housing Administration subsidized mortgages) promised by the federal New Deal. Fortner writes, "Redlining practices limited housing sales, devalued homes, and amplified mortgage failure, resulting in declining neighborhood conditions that increased the risk of lead poisoning and other environmental hazards."[41] Now, almost a century later, "Black Americans are 75% more likely to live in close proximity to oil and gas facilities," resulting in "higher rates of cancer and asthma, [with] Black children twice as likely to develop asthma as their peers."[42]

Not only are residents in redlined communities more likely to develop preventable illness, but the design of their neighborhoods and the lack of trees,[43] coupled with the lack of air conditioning, makes them subject to extreme heat, which exacerbates poor health and affects learning. Hoffman, Shandas, and Pendleton found that 94% of the areas they studied showed elevated land temperatures in formerly redlined areas relative to their non-redlined neighbors:

> No other category of hazardous weather event in the United States has caused more fatalities over the last few decades than extreme heat. In fact, extreme heat is the leading cause of summertime morbidity and has specific impacts on those communities with pre-existing health conditions (e.g., chronic obstructive pulmonary disease, asthma, cardiovascular disease, etc.), limited access to resources, and the elderly. Excess heat limits the human body's ability to regulate its internal temperature, which can result in increased cases of heat cramps, heat exhaustion, and heatstroke and may exacerbate other nervous system, respiratory, cardiovascular, genitourinary, and diabetes-related conditions.

> Urban landscapes amplify extreme heat due to the imbalance of low-slung built surfaces to natural, non-human manufactured landscapes. This urban heat island effect can cause temperatures to vary as much as 10°C within a single urban area.... Emerging research suggests that many of the hottest urban areas also tend to be inhabited by resource-limited residents and communities of color, underscoring the emerging lens of environmental justice as it relates to urban climate change and adaptation.[44]

This is "a result of decades of intentional investment in parks, green spaces, trees, transportation and housing policies that provided 'cooling services,' which also coincide with being wealthier and whiter across the country."[45] As summarized by Dr. Robert Bullard, Distinguished Professor of Urban Planning and Environmental Policy at Texas Southern University, "Zip code is still a potent predictor of health and well-being. . . . Environmental vulnerability maps closely with racial injustice."[46] Educational opportunity, influenced by quality of life, today continues to be shaped by policies and practices rooted in racial discrimination.

Environmental Toxic Stress and Trauma

In addition to direct health threats, previously redlined communities often lack grocery stores, banks, pharmacies, and nearby employment opportunities and, as a result of the stress caused by high unemployment, underinvestment, and stigma, frequently experience high rates of crime and violence. These combined stresses can easily become what is referred to as *toxic stress*. Toxic stress occurs when stress exposure is frequent or prolonged, dysregulating the body's stress response systems and impacting every other body system. The disruption to the neuroendocrine-immune network leads to a prolonged and abnormal cortisol response and a persistent inflammatory state, which leads to greater risks of infection and a variety of health risks, ranging from pulmonary disease to cancer, psychological illness, and now SARS-CoV-2 (known familiarly as COVID-19). The disruption can also create challenges in brain development, learning, and behavior.[47]

As the American Academy of Pediatrics has described, the resulting chronic elevation of stress hormones can disrupt the maturation of children's developing brain architecture and physiology, with major implications for later-life health, learning, and well-being. Trauma and anxiety also deflect focus and attention from educational tasks, impeding concentration and the learning process.[48] As just one example of how this can manifest in school, researchers have found a strong association between students' academic performance and both their subjective assessment of their neighborhood's safety, and an objective assessment of neighborhood environment (the Neighborhood Inventory for Environmental Typology). They found, for example, that neighborhood violence was associated with math and reading achievement decreases, while an increase in perceived safety was associated with corresponding increases in student scores.[49]

Millions of children are grappling with environmental toxins that put stress on their bodies, minds, and spirits, while the adults around them are also weathering the results of years of physical, situational, and psychological stress, under conditions that comprise what Shawn Ginwright calls "persistent traumatic stress environments" (PTSE).[50] Eclipsing post-traumatic stress disorder, PTSE happens when a "post-trauma" state is not possible. Stressors are not solely acute, single moments of trauma—they are atmospheric and ongoing: environmental pollution; food and housing insecurity; the constant threat of neighborhood violence, including from police; and discrimination in schools as well as workplaces.

These contribute to what researchers call adverse childhood experiences, or ACEs. Almost two-thirds of the children in the United States are impacted by ACEs, as each year 46 million children are exposed to violence, crime, abuse, homelessness, or food insecurity, as well as a range of other experiences that cause psychological and physical trauma, such as loss of a family member, divorce, or bullying. These experiences can accumulate as toxic stress that can affect children's attention, learning, and behavior.

Although trauma occurs in every community, poverty and racism, together and separately, make the experience of chronic stress and adversity more likely. Furthermore, in schools where students encounter punitive discipline tactics rather than supports for handling adversity, their stress is magnified.[51]

This isn't just an issue during childhood. The CDC's ACEs resource page lists such potential long-term effects as autoimmune disease, cancer, pulmonary disease, liver disease, memory disturbances, depression, and more. The more ACEs a child experiences, the higher the risk that they will develop a chronic condition later in life.[52] These issues disproportionately impact disabled, Native, Black, immigrant, and LGBTQ+/SGL communities; in other words, those struggling hardest for equitable access to civil and human rights, including education.[53]

Research on human development shows that the effects of such trauma can be mitigated when students learn in a positive school climate that offers long-term, secure relationships that support academic, physical, cognitive, social, and emotional development—an approach known as "whole child" education. Indeed, such an environment boosts achievement for all children, regardless of their circumstances. In addition to meeting basic needs for food and health care, schools can buffer the effects of stress by facilitating supportive adult–child relationships that extend over time; building a sense of self-efficacy and control by teaching and reinforcing social and emotional skills that help children handle adversity, such as the ability to calm emotions and manage responses; and creating dependable, supportive routines for both managing classrooms and checking in on student needs.

THE CIVIL RIGHTS CONTRIBUTION AND ROAD AHEAD

Environmental Justice

Environmental concerns have been the subject of civil rights efforts for decades.[54] Advocacy work that resulted in passage of the Clean Air Act of 1970 began in the 1950s with residents writing countless letters to elected officials, industry officials, and sitting presidents. Along the way, President Eisenhower signed the Air Pollution Control Act of 1955, which was extended in 1959, and Congress passed the Clean Air Act of 1963, then the Motor Vehicle Air Pollution Act of 1965, then the Air Quality Act of 1967. Well-resourced industry lobbyists worked hard to prevent the legislation.[55]

In 1979 Houston residents went to battle with Southwestern Waste Management, Inc., which sought to locate a municipal landfill next to their homes. Research undertaken by the prosecuting attorney's husband, Robert D. Bullard, demonstrated that Black neighborhoods in Houston were overwhelmingly and disproportionately selected as sites of toxic waste disposal.[56] Robert Bullard went on to research, advocate for, and become known as the "father of" what became the environmental justice movement. Offering a historical account of the movement's origins, he wrote:

> The environmental justice movement has come a long way since its humble beginnings in 1982 in Warren County, North Carolina, where a polychlorinated biphenyl (PCB) landfill ignited protests that resulted in over 500 arrests. These protests provided the impetus for a US General Accounting Office study in 1983, *Siting of Hazardous Waste Landfills and Their Correlation with Racial and Economic Status of Surrounding Communities*, [which] revealed that three out of four of the off-site, commercial hazardous waste landfills in the region . . . were located in predominantly African-American communities, although African-Americans made up only 20 per cent of the region's population.

> After waiting more than two decades, an environmental justice victory finally came to the residents of predominately black Warren County. . . . Detoxification work began on the dump in June 2001 and the last clean-up operations were slated to end the latter part of December 2003. State and federal sources spent $18 million to detoxify or neutralize contaminated soil stored at the Warren County PCB landfill.

> The protests also led the Commission for Racial Justice to produce *Toxic Waste and Race* in 1987, the first national study to correlate waste facility sites and demographic characteristics. Race was found to be the most potent variable in predicting where these facilities were located—more powerful than poverty, land values and home ownership.

> In 1990, the book *Dumping in Dixie: Race, Class, and Environmental Quality* chronicled the convergence of two critical social movements, the social justice and environmental movements, into the environmental justice movement. African-American environmental activism emerged initially from the southern United States, the same region that gave birth to the modern civil rights movement. What started out as local, and often isolated, community-based struggles against toxins and hazardous facility siting blossomed into a multi-issue, multi-ethnic and multiregional movement.[57]

There have been gains and losses, and struggles persist to the present day. Title VI of the Civil Rights Act of 1964 prohibited racial discrimination by any entity receiving federal funds, which led to the creation of the Environmental Protection Agency's civil rights office. However, despite persistent, well-documented, and devastating evidence of environmental racism, that office had failed to make a single formal finding of a Title VI violation as recently as 2015.[58] A key complaint during the Flint, MI, lead poisoning fiasco was that the EPA fell well short of its obligations, and in 2017, residents brought suit against the agency.[59] As noted earlier, millions of households continue to be at risk for lead exposure.

It is only now that we see some hope of toxic waste site cleanups through the Biden administration's Infrastructure Investment and Jobs Act, passed in November 2021. The Act includes a $3.5 billion Superfund for this purpose, which is intended to clean up near 50 highly polluted toxic waste sites around the country, and support work at dozens of others across 24 states that have languished for lack of funding.[60] About 60% of the sites to be cleaned up are in low-income communities of color. Current EPA administrator Michael Regan noted: "With this funding, communities living near many of these most serious uncontrolled or abandoned releases of contamination will finally get the protection they deserve." Regan also announced plans to release another $2.9 billion in funds for lead pipe removal nationwide and to impose stricter rules to limit exposure to lead.[61] This is a start on a much larger problem that will take many years, more funding, and sustained resolve to correct.

Elimination of Child Poverty

With some hope on the horizon at the infrastructural level, there is still a crucial need for protections in other areas. Social safety net benefits that should mitigate issues such as unstable housing, food instability, neighborhood violence, and additional challenges associated with precarity are frequently under attack, most recently with the Trump Administration's budget-cutting efforts,[62] and many local, state, and national advocacy organizations have undertaken protests and lawsuits to protect programs like the Supplemental Nutrition Assistance Program, Medicaid, and subsidized housing, access to which impacts millions of school children's daily lives and learning by providing food, housing, and a sense of security, among other things. The fight to secure, protect, and advance these services is not new.

As Americans were pressing the fight for civil rights in the 1960s, President Johnson declared an "unconditional war on poverty." The January 1964 declaration was quickly followed by passage of the Economic Opportunity Act of 1964, which, along with the Civil Rights Act of 1964, set the stage to advance health, education, anti-poverty, and employment policies. In fact, the two pieces of legislation were mutually reinforcing. Martha J. Bailey and Nicolas J. Duquette (2014) describe the immediate aftermath of Johnson's 1964 call to action thus:

> Over the next five years, Congress passed legislation that transformed American schools, launched Medicare and Medicaid, and expanded housing subsidies, urban development programs, employment and training programs, food stamps, and Social Security and welfare benefits. These programs more than tripled real

federal expenditures on health, education, and welfare, which grew to over 15 percent of the federal budget by 1970.[63]

During the 1960s, this set of policies cut the child poverty rate in half. Together with major investments in education for low-income children through the 1965 Elementary and Secondary Education Act and large allocations of aid during the 1970s for school desegregation, teacher recruitment, curriculum improvement, summer programs, and more, the achievement gap between White and Black students was decreased by more than half by the 1980s (see Figure 2.1). Had those policies and the steep slope of change continued, the achievement gap would have been closed by the year 2000.

However, nearly all these programs were eliminated or sharply reduced during the Reagan administration, and the federal education budget was cut in half. Early in his presidency, the administration cut housing subsidies, food stamps, Pell Grants, student loans, and unemployment compensation. Children were cut off from food benefits, including three million who lost school lunch, one million who lost food stamps, and 500,000 who were cut from school breakfast programs. Approximately 750,000 children lost Medicaid benefits, and more than 300,000 families lost access to public housing. Hunger and homelessness rose dramatically. [64]

Achievement for Black and Hispanic students declined, and the achievement gap grew as childhood poverty increased and educational investments shrank. The gap remains now, over 30 years later, 30 percent greater than it was in 1988.[65]

Although the Clinton administration restored some federal support for family benefits, helping to reduce child poverty in the early 1990s, in his second term Clinton advanced the Personal Responsibility and Work Opportunity Reconciliation Act with the slogan *Welfare to Work*. In a job-starved economy, people already struggling to survive were expected to find work, at abysmally low wages, as benefits receded, and mothers raising small children were expected to do so without access to affordable day care. Aid to Families with Dependent Children was replaced by a system of temporary, time-limited aid to be administered by states, and federal funding was reduced by $54 billion. This effectively eliminated the social safety net for people experiencing deep poverty.

While government benefits have made a difference in poverty reduction over the years,[66] to this day, nearly 1 in 5 American children live in poverty—one of the highest rates in the industrialized world.[67] Further, 5 million of them (roughly 7% of all U.S. children) live in deep poverty, at less than half the poverty line threshold, which is $27,750 for a family of four.[68] Living in a family with income of less than $14,000 per year means frequently living without food, safe shelter, health care, and many of the other basic necessities of survival.[69] Such a life also comes with many other risks. For example, the percentage of young children in deep poverty who have elevated lead levels is over 17 times higher than the percentage for non-poor children.[70] Recent research shows that deep poverty is associated with the re-emergence of diseases

Figure 2.1. Trends in Reading Scores for 13-Year-Olds on the National Assessment of Educational Progress

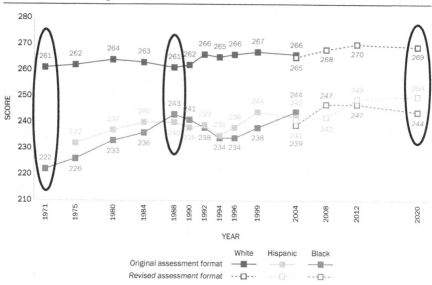

Source: The Nation's Report Card (n.d.). *National assessment of educational progress long-term trend assessment results: Reading.* https://www.nationsreportcard.gov/ltt /reading/student-group-scores/?age=13

thought to be eradicated, declining life expectancies, and nearly constant food and housing security.[71] As a result of the tattered safety net and rising costs of living, more than 1.5 million children enrolled in public schools and more than 1.3 million under the age of 6 were homeless in 2017–2018.[72]

An important advance was made in the Biden administration with the American Rescue Plan Act, passed in 2021 to deal with the effects of the COVID-19 pandemic, which includes an array of policies aimed at reducing poverty through income transfers associated with a family child tax credit, as well as health and child care benefits, nutrition assistance, and housing supports. The Act cut the rate of child poverty by more than half in 2021, with the greatest benefits for Black and Latinx children and families.[73] The Biden Administration's Build Back Better framework would have extended the tax credit, along with housing and health care supports that would begin to rebuild a safety net. However, the failure of the Senate to pass this bill has left in limbo the future of this critically important anti-poverty agenda. The expiration of the child tax credit in December 2021 increased child poverty overnight from 12% to 17% by January 2022—another devastating blow to families living at the edge of survival.[74]

Clearly, the civil rights road ahead must continue to pursue policies that rebuild the tattered safety net for children and families and eliminate child poverty. It must also feature ongoing litigation and legislation to eliminate toxins in the environment and to rebuild communities that have been cordoned off from investment and opportunity, so that their children can thrive. In order to support optimal conditions for development and learning, the schools that children attend in these communities must also be well supported. Notably, this includes adequate and equitable resources for schools themselves, a prerequisite for deeper learning and an area of civil rights advocacy that we take up in the next chapter.

CHAPTER 3

Well-Resourced School Systems

If Hispanic and African American student performance grew to be comparable to White performance and remained there over the next 80 years, the . . . impact would be staggering—adding some $50 trillion (in present value terms) to our economy. This [is] more than three times the size of our current GDP [gross domestic product] and represents the income that we forgo by not ensuring equity for all of our students.

—*For Each and Every Child*, Report of the Excellence and Equity Commission[1]

THE LONG-TERM FIGHT FOR ADEQUATE AND EQUITABLE SCHOOL RESOURCES

Challenges in the creation of educational opportunity are as old as the nation itself.[2] *Brown v. Board of Education* and its precedent cases illustrate that not all people have been considered worthy of a high-quality education across American history.[3] School segregation and unequal funding have always gone hand in hand. Indeed, institutionally sanctioned discrimination in access to education is older than America itself. In his history of 18th-century colonial education, Lawrence Cremin wrote:

> For all of its openness, provincial America . . . distributed its educational resources unevenly, and to some groups, particularly those Indians and Afro-Americans who were enslaved and even those who were not, it was for all intents and purposes closed. . . . For the slaves, there were few books, few libraries, [and] few schools. . . . The doors of wisdom were not only not open, they were shut tight and designed to remain that way. . . . By the end of the colonial period, there was a well-developed ideology of race inferiority to justify that situation and ensure that it would stand firm against all the heady rhetoric of the Revolution.[4]

The legacy of discrimination did persist. From the time Southern states made it illegal to teach an enslaved person to read, throughout the 19th century and into the 20th, Black communities faced de facto and de jure exclusion from public schools throughout the nation, as did Native and Mexican American populations. In the North, the problems were also severe: "While [19th century] publicists glorified the unifying influence of common learning

28

under the common roof of the common school, [Black] Americans were rarely part of that design."[5]

Many of the cases leading up to *Brown* focused on the huge inequalities in funding for schools serving Black and White children, but ultimately, it was the decision to focus on desegregation, rather than funding equity, that helped move the *Brown* case to success.[6] Since the decision in 1954, advocates have leveraged it to fight for, and sometimes win, the advances in educational opportunity made possible by a well-resourced school system. But both unequal resources and high levels of racial and economic segregation persist.

The progress made in the 1960s and 1970s with the War on Poverty, coupled with desegregation enforcement, efforts to equalize resources, and large investments in cities and low-income schools, made a substantial difference in the quality of schools available to students of color. During this era, the gap between Black and White students in reading achievement decreased by more than half in reading and by about one third in mathematics. Financial aid for higher education also sharply increased, especially for need-based scholarships and loans. For a brief period in the mid-1970s, Black and Latinx students attended college at the same rate as White students—the only time this occurred before or since.[7]

But all these gains were quickly rolled back. With President Nixon's removal of "administrative enforcement" in 1968 and his appointment of four conservative Supreme Court judges came "the first divided desegregation decisions since *Brown*."[8] The *Milliken v. Bradley* decision undermined *Brown* in Detroit, reinforced by housing segregation, racial disenfranchisement, and White flight. "This phenomenon," Khiara Bridges notes, "played out in school districts around the country." She writes, "In essence, courts began ending judicial oversight of school boards on the finding that continuing efforts to desegregate schools would be tough—not on the finding that school boards actually had successfully desegregated their schools."[9] And as Figure 3.1 vividly shows, resegregation occurred rapidly in the districts where judicial oversight was terminated.

Segregation and poverty go hand in hand, with a growing number of schools serving concentrations of low-income students, more that 90% of whom are students of color, generally Black, Latinx, Pacific Islander, and/or Native American.[10] And in most states, these schools receive less funding than those serving more advantaged students. According to the Education Law Center's most recent analysis, only nine states have "progressive" funding systems that allocate at least 10% more per-pupil funding to high-poverty districts than to low-poverty districts. Others offer little support to meet these students' needs, and at least 20 states spend between 3% and 32% less on high-poverty than low-poverty districts.[11] And within school districts, schools serving children from low-income families and students of color often get less funding than those serving more affluent students.[12] This is particularly true of the growing number of "apartheid schools"—those serving more than 90% students of color who are also from low-income families—which are generally severely underresourced and struggling to close academic gaps while underwriting the additional costs of

Figure 3.1. Degree of Segregation in Relation to Court-Ordered Desegregation Plans

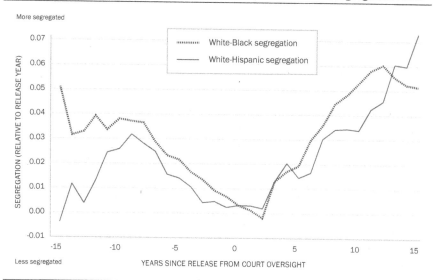

Source: Darling-Hammond, L. (2018). *Education and the path to one nation, indivisible.* Learning Policy Institute. Figure developed from data in Reardon, S., Grewal, E. T., Kalogrides, D., & Greenberg, E. (2012). *Brown* fades: The end of court-ordered school desegregation and the resegregation of American public schools. *Journal of Policy Analysis and Management, 31*(4), 876–904.

addressing the effects of poverty: hunger, homelessness, and other traumas experienced by children and families in chronically underserved communities.[13] Left with larger class sizes and without a wide range of needed services both inside and outside the classroom, apartheid schools typically also feature a revolving door of underprepared teachers whose lack of training and high attrition rates depress students' achievement levels further.

HOW SCHOOL FINANCE INFLUENCES OPPORTUNITIES FOR DEEPER LEARNING

It is not always clear how school funding influences not just the quantity of resources but also the very nature of the education students receive. The 30 years of litigation and nine court decisions in New Jersey that occurred between the late 1960s, when the *Robinson v. Cahill* lawsuit was first brought, and 1998, when the state finally began to equalize spending, provide a vivid example. The state legislature's response to the first court decision in 1973 preserved the local taxing authority and large inequalities in spending. It promised "thorough and efficient" education through lengthy checklists and monitoring activities designed to ensure districts could demonstrate that they were implementing state regulations and a minimum basic skills curriculum, evaluated through state tests.[14] Paradoxically, this approach to "equity" deflected resources away from classroom instruction and toward the hiring of bureaucrats to manage the elaborate planning, inspection, and reporting systems—a luxury the starving city schools could ill afford.

In 1976, New Jersey State Education Commissioner Fred Burke expressed the view that has often surfaced in state resistance to equalization of funding: "Urban children, even after years of remediation, will not be able to perform in school as well as their suburban counterparts. . . . We are just being honest."[15] These kinds of statements have appeared in many state defenses of their inequitable school finance systems to justify the status quo.

As Jean Anyon notes, "During the next two decades [after 1973], the cities, which were closely monitored by the state, did offer a basic skills curriculum to students, while the suburbs continued to offer sophisticated curriculum programs and a range of courses."[16] As plaintiffs noted in one round of litigation in the 1980s, the wealthy and predominantly White Montclair school district offered foreign languages at the preschool level, while the poor and predominantly Black district in the city of Paterson did not offer any until high school—and then, relatively few. And while 20% of 11th- and 12th-graders in wealthy Moorestown participated in Advanced Placement courses, none were even offered in any school in poor and predominantly Black Camden and East Orange.[17]

Along the way, inequalities in spending grew, with rich districts such as Princeton spending twice as much as some poor, and virtually all-Black, districts had available. Responding to a second lawsuit that was brought in 1981 and finally decided in 1990, the state argued that funding to poorer districts should not be increased because it might be mismanaged and wasted and that "money is not a critical factor in the quality of education in the first place."[18] Such resources as course offerings, teacher experience and education, and class sizes or pupil-teacher ratios, the state suggested, were not reliable indicators of the quality of education. Such quality could be better evaluated through the monitoring of the implementation of state regulations and mandates, a massive bureaucratic activity that consumed reams of paper but did little to ensure high-quality teaching in classrooms. The state further argued that these urban, minority students did not need the same kind or quality of education as those in wealthy suburbs:

> The [basic skills] education currently offered in these poorer urban districts is tailored to the students' present need. . . . These students simply cannot now benefit from the kind of vastly superior course offerings found in the richer districts.[19]

In its 1990 decision, the Court explicitly rejected these arguments, replying that it did not believe that students in poorer districts were less deserving of a rich curriculum or less able to benefit from one. Although the Court once again found the state funding system unconstitutional, it would be another decade before large infusions of funds would find their way into the by-then dysfunctional urban districts after yet another major lawsuit had been brought. While New Jersey lawmakers were avoiding responsibility for paying for the education of students of color from low-income families, here is how the state education department described the education of students in Newark in 1994:

> Children in the Newark public schools . . . endure degrading school environments that virtually ensure academic failure. . . . [In many classrooms], there is nothing. . . . Science laboratories lack basic equipment. [Students], with rare exceptions, sit dutifully in rows, filling in the blanks in workbooks with answers to items having to do with isolated skills, or listening to a teacher deliver facts or talk about skills, divorced from meaningful context. . . . Seldom in any class observed, no matter what the grade level or subject, were students being taught how to write, how to read for understanding, how to solve problems, or how to think critically.

> Physical conditions in most of the schools . . . reveal neglect. . . . Holes in floors and walls; dirty classrooms with blackboards so worn as to be unusable; filthy lavatories without toilet paper, soap, or paper towels; inoperable water fountains . . . and foul-smelling effluent running from a school into the street speak of disregard . . . for students and teachers. . . . A virtual army of supervisors, administrators, and coordinators holds all this in place, passing various . . . forms from one layer of bureaucracy to the next, while schools go unpainted for as long as 14 years, and in classroom after classroom, whole banks of lights are without fluorescent tubes or light shields.

> These conditions tell of shocking neglect. Equally shocking, however, is the lack of indignation on the part of staff. One teacher interviewed explained it this way: "After a while," she said, looking around, "you lower your expectations."[20]

A decade later the same arguments were heard in similar litigation in California, where the state's cities were typically funded at half the level of the wealthiest districts. The plaintiffs' brief in the *Williams v. State of California* (2000) lawsuit included this description of a school serving low-income students of color in San Francisco:

> At Luther Burbank, students cannot take textbooks home for homework in any core subject. . . . Some math, science, and other core classes do not have even enough textbooks for all the students in a single class to use during the school day, so some students must share the same one book during class time. . . . For homework, students must take home photocopied pages, with no accompanying text for guidance or reference, when and if their teachers have enough paper to use to make homework copies. . . . The social studies textbook Luther Burbank students use is so old that it does not reflect the breakup of the former Soviet Union. Luther Burbank is infested with vermin and roaches and students routinely see mice in their classrooms. One dead rodent has remained, decomposing, in a corner in the gymnasium since

the beginning of the school year. The school library is rarely open, has no librarian, and has not recently been updated. Luther Burbank classrooms do not have computers. Computer instruction and research skills are not, therefore, part of Luther Burbank students' regular instruction in their core courses. . . . Two of the three bathrooms at Luther Burbank are locked all day, every day. The third bathroom is locked during lunch and other periods during the school day, so there are times during school when no bathroom at all is available for students to use. Students have urinated or defecated on themselves at school because they could not get into an unlocked bathroom. . . . When the bathrooms are not locked, they often lack toilet paper, soap, and paper towels, and the toilets frequently are clogged and overflowing. . . . Ceiling tiles are missing and cracked in the school gym, and school children are afraid to play basketball and other games in the gym because they worry that more ceiling tiles will fall on them during their games. . . . Eleven of the 35 teachers at Luther Burbank have not yet obtained regular, nonemergency credentials, and 17 of the 35 teachers only began teaching at Luther Burbank this school year.[21]

Eric Hanushek, an expert witness for the defense, argued that more money would not be a useful solution in this case, claiming "There is no evidence that the added resources [devoted to education in the United States over the 20th century] have improved student performance."[22]

Meanwhile, when asked what her ideal school would be, a California high school student testifying for the plaintiffs reflected the lowered expectations we described in New Jersey's cities:

[My ideal school] would be a classroom with enough tables, enough chairs, enough books, enough materials, and a teacher who cares, not just someone who got a GED or whatever. . . . Enough supplies, enough security, and just enough everything. . . . Just because we're smaller, we are still human beings.

Deeper learning is not possible when the funding for a rich curriculum taught by well-prepared teachers with supportive materials is absent—and when the official government view is that large numbers of students do not need or deserve such a curriculum.

THE CIVIL RIGHTS CONTRIBUTION AND ROAD AHEAD

Equalizing School Funding

In 1965, Arthur Wise published an article challenging the constitutionality of school finance schemes that produce radically disparate per-pupil expenditures within states.[23] Arguing that such unequal spending leads to unequal educational opportunities, he suggested that this might constitute a denial by the state of equal protection under the law. A number of lawsuits were filed on these grounds, and the first major success occurred in 1973, when the New Jersey

Supreme Court declared, in *Robinson v. Cahill,* that the state's school financing system was in violation of the New Jersey Constitution's Education Clause, which called for a "thorough and efficient system of free public schools" for all children between the ages of 5 and 18. In that same year, however, the United States Supreme Court rejected an argument in a Texas case, *San Antonio Independent School District vs. Rodriguez,*[24] that education constitutes a fundamental right under the federal Constitution. This cut off further federal court challenges of educational funding inequities.

Because education is a state responsibility outlined in each state constitution, litigation to address inequalities has occurred in virtually every state at some time over the past 50 years with very different results across the states, even when the extent of inequalities was quite similar. In some states, cases have been brought repeatedly, arguing that there is an unmet constitutional obligation to ensure equitable access to a "sound basic education," "a thorough and efficient education," or whatever descriptor the state constitution requires.[25]

In total, courts in ten of the thirty-one states where suits were filed during the 1970s and early 1980s found their state's school finance scheme to be unconstitutional.[26] This series of state challenges was followed by a decade of little activity. One reason for this was the dismantling of federal and state databases that had been used to document disparities. During the Reagan administration, some federal data collection and reporting that allowed analysis of inequalities was discontinued, and the federal funding that had supported data collection by state departments of education was also ended.

These data systems have been gradually rebuilt. Today, the data about school disparities that support ongoing litigation is a function of federally required data systems at both the federal level (for example, the Civil Rights Data Collection and the Common Core of Data) and at the state level (for example, district- and school-level funding data required under ESSA).

As noted earlier, only nine states have progressive funding systems that spend at least 10% more on children in high-poverty districts than on those in more affluent districts. A much greater number make no additional investment or even have regressive systems that spend more on the education of students in more affluent districts.[27]

However, following litigation, those states that have substantially equalized their funding systems have seen dramatic improvements in learning and achievement. For example, Massachusetts climbed to the number 1 rank in student achievement on the National Assessment of Educational Progress in the 1990s after it enacted school funding reforms that added money for students in poverty, English learners, and those identified for special education—coupled with investments in new standards, assessments, extensive teacher training, and preschool for students from low-income families.[28] It overtook Connecticut, which had several years earlier increased resources and equalized spending by investing heavily in high and equitable teacher salaries and in training for teachers and principals, reducing achievement gaps and catapulting the state to the leading status in the country, before it was overtaken by Massachusetts.[29] These comprehensive approaches to funding had positive effects on student performance in both states.

Massachusetts has maintained its top-ranked status for student achievement for more than 30 years, since the late 1990s, although it is now challenged by New Jersey, which undertook similar reforms several years later following the 30-year court battle described above. The plaintiff districts—cities largely serving students of color from low-income families—received "parity funding" with wealthy suburban districts that were previously spending nearly twice as much, high-quality preschool for all 3- and 4-year-olds, and extensive teacher training in literacy and mathematics, and engaged in whole-school redesign models. Now a "majority–minority" state, with 53% of its students being students of color, New Jersey ranks number 1 or 2 in the country on every indicator of achievement and attainment. In all of these states, these investments resulted from litigation directed at unequal funding and, in several cases, at segregation as well.[30]

As fights for integration and equal access to resources have persisted, they have achieved important outcomes. A large-scale national study found that districts that substantially increased spending in response to court-ordered school finance reforms saw significant increases among students from low-income families in high school graduation, followed by higher wages and lower poverty rates as adults.[31]

Fighting for Integration

Researchers have also shown significant benefits from court-ordered desegregation. As economist Rucker Johnson found, during the era of federally enforced desegregation, Black children achieved more and graduated at higher rates when they experienced desegregated schools, and the longer they were in these schools, the greater the associated gains. For example, Black students' graduation rates climbed by 2 percentage points for every year they attended an integrated school, and exposure to court-ordered desegregation for all 12 years of school completely closed the Black–White attainment gap while substantially raising wages and reducing poverty in adulthood, with no negative impact on White student outcomes.[32]

A large body of literature discusses both the negative effects of segregation and the positive effects of desegregation on student achievement. For example, a review of research on mathematics achievement found—across 59 studies—that "mathematics outcomes are likely to be higher for students from all grade levels, racial, and SES [socioeconomic status] backgrounds who attend racially and socioeconomically integrated schools."[33]

Desegregated settings have also been found to promote critical elements of deeper learning. A synthesis of 4 decades of research found that the academic benefits for students of color of attending diverse schools include not only higher achievement in math, science, language, and reading and higher graduation and college-going rates, but also—for all students—enhanced social and historical thinking, critical problem-solving, collaboration, and intergroup relationships, all of which provide students with the interpersonal skills they need in the globalizing economy.[34]

But achieving these gains, even today, requires constant vigilance and civil rights enforcement, as schools have resegregated since the 1980s. Federal efforts were critical in advancing integrated schools, starting in the 1960s, through court action, legislated incentives, and funding for integration. Whereas only 1% of Black children in the South attended schools with White children in 1963, approximately 90% of Black children attended desegregated schools in the early 1970s. This number peaked in the late 1980s, when not only did most Black students attend desegregated schools, but 44% attended majority-White schools. Today that proportion is only about 20%.[35] Meanwhile, about 40% of schools are intensely segregated, half of them serving more than 90% White students and half of them serving more than 90% students of color.[36]

This is largely because many federal administrations since the early 1960s have worked to limit and undo remedies for integrating schools. For example, Richard Nixon put a stop to federal enforcement of desegregation orders in 1968 and appointed four conservative justices to the Supreme Court who ended many desegregation rulings. The federal desegregation aid that had enabled districts to work on strategies to improve intergroup relations and finance integration efforts was cancelled in President Reagan's first budget.[37]

As courts encountered requests to end desegregation orders, the federal government often weighed in on the side of districts seeking to end desegregation, as the Bush Administration did in the *Parents Involved in Community Schools v. Seattle School District No. 1* lawsuit, decided by the Supreme Court in 2007. This case challenged the efforts of the Seattle School District to assign students in ways that would create racially integrated schools. In striking down the Seattle plan, the Supreme Court noted that considerations of race cannot be used to achieve mere "racial balancing" and can only be considered as part of a "broader effort to achieve 'exposure to widely diverse people, cultures, ideas, and viewpoints.'"[38] Following the Supreme Court's ruling, the Bush administration issued a "Dear Colleague" letter narrowly interpreting the case as prohibiting any consideration of race in school assignments, going even further than the Court had gone in undermining voluntary, race-conscious student assignment strategies.

While the Obama administration issued guidance to clarify how districts could constitutionally continue with voluntary desegregation plans, that guidance was rescinded by the Trump administration. One account in 2017 noted that the Trump administration might complete what the Bush administration started. Of the 430 school districts under court order to desegregate in 2000, nearly two-thirds were no longer under an obligation to do so:

> During George W. Bush's administration, almost 200 districts shed their court orders. With just 176 districts left, Trump's Justice Department could bring an end to the 63-year-old effort to erase the legacy of Jim Crow in the

American education system, at a time when nearly 8.4 million black and Latino children are learning in segregated and high-poverty schools.[39]

The road ahead will require a number of efforts to end the legacy of under-resourced and segregated schools:

- Ongoing school finance reform litigation and legislation at the state level to achieve policies that provide funding based on pupil needs—including poverty, homelessness, English learner status, and special education status—rather than as a function of property tax wealth in local communities;
- Reinstatement of the federal guidance from the Departments of Education and Justice to states and localities about how to support school diversity and of technical assistance from the Office of Civil Rights to aid in program implementation and to help ensure compliance with civil rights laws;
- Re-engagement of federal support for desegregation through investments in such programs as the Magnet Schools Assistance Program, organized not only to support individual schools and districts but also to enable states to pursue interdistrict solutions to segregation, like those in Connecticut, Massachusetts, and Nebraska.[40]

Creating Supportive Learning Environments

To get to deeper learning possibilities, systems of schooling not only must become more equitable in their allocation of funds, but also must invest in early education, teacher quality, teacher learning, academic standards focused on deeper learning skills, and high-quality curriculum, as we describe in subsequent chapters. This is the kind of investment that provides student access and support, teacher development and retention, curricular innovation, and responsiveness to the changing world.

There is yet another set of actions needed to create equity within schools, even when they have been adequately resourced. These include treating students of color with the respect and care that support positive whole-child development. The complex set of issues associated with this struggle can be seen in the challenges to students of color that initially occurred and continue to occur in many desegregated schools. Even with a Supreme Court mandate, desegregation was not without costs. As Khiara Bridges noted:

> For black children, desegregation meant being plucked out of all-black environments that, while underfunded relative to their counterparts, were supportive and nurturing. Instead of learning in friendly and warm black schools, black children were being placed into unfriendly and unwelcoming white spaces [and] when black students were sent to white schools, the predominantly black schools that they

previously had attended usually were closed. Black teachers, administrators, and principals—folks who had dedicated their lives to educating black children—lost their jobs and their livelihoods.

These facts led many . . . to question whether they should have tried a different approach. They speculated whether, instead of fighting for school integration, they ought to have fought for the equalization of black and white schools. [This] position . . . obviated the need to plead to white schools to accept black children, saved black children from environments whose hostility was both overt and subtle, and would result in a self-sufficient, empowered black community. However, many found the position disquieting. For them, it sounded too much like a capitulation to *Plessy v. Ferguson*'s pronouncement of "separate but equal. . . ." Moreover, many others doubted that equalizing black and white schools would result in black children achieving the same educational outcomes as their white counterparts.[41]

As Bridges observes, the imbalance that was created by losing so many Black educators supporting Black students in safe spaces has often undermined learning for Black and brown children who need culturally sustaining experiences. In today's context, efforts to improve all the schools that students of color attend must include both the equalization of resources and the humanization of the school environment so that every child experiences physical and psychological safety as well as inclusion and the opportunity to learn in empowering ways that support student agency and success. We turn to these issues in the next chapter.

CHAPTER 4

Supportive and Inclusive Schools

I dropped out of school—actually they kicked me out because I didn't want to give them my hat. It was real zero tolerance! I was expelled for defiance for putting a hat in my backpack instead of giving it to them. And I had had bad experiences since preschool so it was easy for me to be like "[Forget] this." As a teenager, I was thinking, "You don't care about us anyway. You just get paid checks per student in a seat."

—Darius Robinson (pseudonym)[1]

WHY POSITIVE SCHOOL CLIMATE MATTERS

From the community to the classroom, children's developmental contexts matter a great deal. Their cognitive, physical, and social–emotional development are intertwined, which means that threats to one threaten the other.[2] A synthesis of research on the educational implications of the science of learning and development confirms that:

- Learning is social, emotional, and academic. Relationships matter—profoundly. When they are positive, they open the mind to learning. When they are negative, they dampen the brain's processing power. A child's best performance occurs under conditions of high support and low threat.
- Supportive, responsive human relationships are the essential ingredient that catalyzes healthy development and learning. Adults who are warm, consistent, and attuned to students support positive brain development, even buffering children against other sources of adversity.
- Human development is variable and unique to each individual. Children develop skills and understandings at different rates across domains based on their prior experiences and contexts. To support their growth, curriculum and instruction need to attend to the developmental trajectory of each child.
- Development is malleable and continuous across a person's life span. It responds to key inputs like relationships, social

interactions, and contexts, and domains of development interact.
Changes in one domain affect others. Families, schools, and society
are all influences.

- Adversity affects learning—and the way schools respond matters. A
  child suffering excess stress may suffer physiological effects, anxiety,
  depression, lack of focus, and difficulty with memory and executive
  functioning. Schools can help to relieve these challenges or may
  reinforce them. Implicit bias, stereotyping, punitive discipline, and
  exclusion, all of which disproportionately affect marginalized students,
  become additional sources of trauma for children who are already
  suffering. On the other hand, caring adults and wraparound supports
  can be sources of resilience and healing.[3]

Education aims both to cultivate the conditions for learning that enable
every child's academic success and to support children's lifelong opportunities.
As we noted earlier, children learn when they feel supported and safe. Their
learning can be impaired when they are fearful, anxious, or traumatized.[4] As
Jennings and Greenberg note in a review of research:

> [Research] supports this view—that students learn better when they are happy,
> respected, and feel cared for, feel bonded to school, trust the people at school
> have their best interests at heart, and have high levels of self-efficacy.[5]

These conditions are shaped in large part by a school's *climate*—that is,
the way in which students, educators, and families experience the environment.
A school's climate sets the tone at a school and can be seen in the physical
environment, experienced during the learning process, and felt in how people
within the school interact with each other.[6] According to the National School
Climate Center (NSCC):

> School climate is based on patterns of students', parents' and school personnel's
> experience of school life; it also reflects norms, goals, values, interpersonal rela-
> tionships, teaching and learning practices, and organizational structures.[7]

A review of 78 studies found strong influences of these features on student
attendance and achievement and concluded that a positive school climate can
mitigate the negative effects of poverty on academic performance. This occurs,
most importantly, through teachers and other staff who show support, acceptance, and warmth.[8]

Accomplishing these outcomes for students hinges on the environments
adults create for them. For example, the ability to take intellectual risks and
welcome failure in the service of growth (elements of a growth mindset[9]) is
built on a foundation of affirmation, mastery experiences, psychological safety, and a sense of connectedness within the community. Thus, it is important
for schools to be learning environments that offer the security and support

to maximize students' abilities to learn social–emotional skills as well as academic content.

Yet many students do not experience a secure and caring climate, especially in secondary schools. For example, a 2006 study of more than 148,000 6th- to 12th-graders reported the following findings: Only 29% of the students felt their schools provided a caring, encouraging environment. Fewer than half of the students reported they had developed social competencies such as empathy, decision-making skills, and conflict-resolution skills (from 29% to 45%, depending on the competency). Thirty percent of high school students reported engaging in multiple high-risk behaviors, such as substance abuse, sex, violence, and attempted suicide.[10]

Considerable work is needed to create positive learning environments in many schools.

HOW SCHOOL CLIMATE IS CONSTRUCTED

The National School Climate Center delineates 13 dimensions of school climate, including support for learning (supportive teaching practices) and school connectedness. NSCC's school climate dimensions include a sense of physical security as well as a sense of social–emotional security. Without these, students are more likely to avoid school,[11] can suffer diminished cognitive capacity,[12] and can have difficulty cultivating the sense of belonging that enables confidence in the classroom.

The power adults have over learning environments is well studied. In particular, principal and teacher attitudes and behaviors, especially as these are reflected in their relationships with students, are critical.[13] For example, positive teacher attitudes toward working with students with disabilities are associated with higher levels of inclusive practice.[14] School principals set the tone by "communicating clear expectations of an inclusive ethos to staff, providing them with appropriate support and training, and promoting a collective sense of efficacy."[15] A number of studies indicate that this sense of efficacy and the learning climate it supports are stronger when leadership is inclusive and empowers stakeholders.[16]

A strong exemplar of these findings is the Comer School Development Program (SDP). Created by child psychiatrist James Comer, the program identifies two key objectives for educators: "Developing a comprehensive understanding of what needs to be done in the best interests of every child, and then making the deliberate effort to meet the needs of every child effectively."[17]

The model centers six developmental pathways (see Figure 4.1) that attend to children's physical, cognitive, psychological, social, ethical, and language development. A school environment in which students are physically and psychologically safe is the necessary foundation for attending to children's developmental needs as a whole. The program engages all stakeholders—parents, students, community members, teachers, staff, and administrators—to think

Figure 4.1. The Six Developmental Pathways, Comer School Development Program

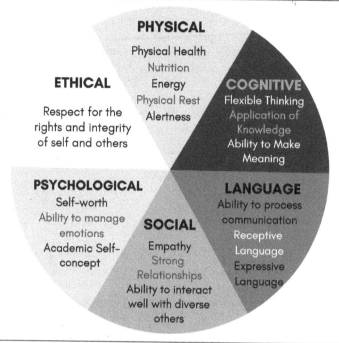

Source: Adapted from Joyner, E. T., Comer, J. P., and Ben-Avie, M. (2004). *Comer schools in action: The 3-volume field guide.* Corwin Press.

about every facet of schooling through a developmental lens and to support child development with both an understanding of the process and explicit opportunities to engage feelings and learn new behaviors.

These efforts are guided by three principles for the work that adults do together: (1) collaboration, (2) consensus, and (3) no-fault problem-solving. Teachers lead classroom meetings and teach social, emotional, and cognitive skills. Families are invited into the school and participate in structured social events, governance, and support for their children so that the home and school are joined in partnership with a common frame of reference for how to collaborate.

The Comer framework asserts that because behavior is a response to perceptions of one's environment, changing behavior requires understanding not only the individual's experiences, feelings, and interpretations, but also the shape of all the environments they inhabit.[18] Darling-Hammond and colleagues offer this elaboration: "A child may sleep in class for reasons that are physical (lack of sleep), cognitive (boredom with the task), or psychological (to disguise feelings of inadequacy). The pathway approach encourages considering multiple causes and generating solutions without blame to address the needs of each child holistically."[19] The SDP's emphasis on broad stakeholder involvement acknowledges that people's growth and well-being are socially mediated. In many studies, schools undertaking SDP with fidelity have experienced improved attendance, achievement, and school climate outcomes.[20]

SCHOOL CLIMATE AND DEEPER LEARNING

As the example of the School Development Program illustrates, to design supportive environments and differentiate supports in response to each student's needs, adults need to model and teach social–emotional skills. The classroom environment is strengthened by explicit attention to social and emotional learning (SEL), that is, "the process through which children and adults understand and manage emotions, set and achieve positive goals, feel and show empathy for others, establish and maintain positive relationships, and make responsible decisions."[21] Two meta-analyses of SEL curriculum programs, examining hundreds of studies, have shown that participating students demonstrate improvements in their social–emotional skills; attitudes about themselves, others, and school; social and classroom behavior; and grades and test scores; and that these outcomes endure for many years.[22]

According to Christina Cipriano, Director of Research at the Yale Center for Emotional Intelligence, these competencies underscore people's "ability to be available to learn and available to teach."[23] She adds:

> If we're not able to regulate or down-regulate in a given situation, we're not able to be available to process the information of what we're being taught. So, regardless of how fantastic your teacher may be or how incredible that science curriculum is at engaging and motivating you, if you have a student who's dealing with stress or trauma or [who is] unable to kind of get over the interpersonal interaction they had right before they entered that classroom or the trigger word that the teacher said, like "pop quiz," that set them off into a spiral, they're not going to be able to process the dynamic curriculum that's being presented to them.[24]

In many schools with explicit attention to social and emotional learning, a key opportunity to process feelings and experiences occurs in the morning. For example, at the Davis Street Magnet School in New Haven, CT, which serves students in grades K–8, students participate in morning meetings that are foundational to the Comer School Development Program process. This daily school structure is a routine that brings consistency while offering opportunities for relationship and skill building that further build the school community and culture.

Several 4th- and 5th-grade students described the impact of the morning meetings in their own words:

> Morning meeting means a lot to me because it helps me with my day. If I had a problem, like yesterday afternoon, I can bring it up to the class and I can go

face-to-face with the person to tell them how I felt about the problem that we had. And it means a lot because it's taught me the ethical pathway, how to talk to people so you don't hurt their feelings when you're asking them to do something or to give them anything.—Rachel

You get to interact with other people and tell them what you feel instead of bubbling up and keeping it inside and then it hurts. But you get to let it out and nobody blames you or says "no I didn't" or stuff like that. Instead, you get to tell them what's wrong, and you get to work it out.—Brianna

I think morning meeting is good because it helps kids with their problems. Like for me, it helped me a lot this year. I used to be getting into a lot of trouble. But then when I learned the Comer pathways, I kind of changed a little. Last year I was getting into trouble and stuff, so now I don't. . . . [The pathways that have helped me] are the cognitive, the language, and the social. I learned how to think before I act.—Shemar

Morning meetings have taught these students how to articulate the stresses that preoccupy them—stresses that could otherwise undermine their learning and disrupt their behavior. In addition, the meetings have helped establish a safe environment that recognizes and values each of them as an important member of the classroom community worthy of having voice.[25]

Being able to recognize emotions, calm oneself, focus attention, and reach out for help are all social–emotional skills essential for learning. These skills are especially needed to sustain effort during the kinds of challenging inquiry tasks associated with deeper learning. Extended research projects, for example, typically require significant productive struggle in the course of problem-solving. To be motivated to try, students need both the growth mindset and the social–emotional tools of resilience and perseverance that allow them to undertake difficult tasks and take risks. These tools are acquired in classrooms where students have a strong sense of membership and belonging, where their value and competence is affirmed, and where they are taught both how to work independently and how to problem-solve with others to overcome obstacles that are part of the learning process.[26]

Educators enacting a whole-child experience work to attach children to the school community, ensure that they feel a sense of belonging, and teach them how to be a contributing member of that community while eschewing punitive and exclusionary discipline to the greatest degree possible. Studies show that when schools help students form social bonds with adults and with each other, disciplinary problems are reduced.[27] Nevertheless, exclusion through segregated classrooms, as well as through suspensions and expulsions, has been a staple element in school practice since zero-tolerance and "no excuses" policies became widespread in the 1980s. Over the past 2 decades, civil rights enforcement has been essential to pave a path toward inclusive school practices for students of color and students with disabilities, as we discuss below. Similar efforts have been and are critical for students who are sexual orientation- and/ or gender-expansive, undocumented, unhoused, fostered, and incarcerated.

SCHOOL EXCLUSION AND DISCRIMINATION

School climate and experiences of support and belonging can diverge substantially within a school for students from different racial and ethnic, income, language, disability, gender, and sexual orientation groups. A number of studies have found, for example, that students of color perceive fewer positive school experiences—for example, fewer favorable experiences of safety, connectedness, relationships with adults, and opportunities for participation—in comparison to their White peers.[28]

Students experience numerous forms of exclusion and discrimination in school and the larger society. In some cases, they or their experiences are made invisible because they fall outside of a normative mainstream. LGBTQIA+ histories and icons are absent from curricula; Native lives and contributions are frozen in some distant, whitewashed past—their present erased and ignored; Black, Latinx, and Asian stories are tokenized; students with disabilities are segregated away from their peers and rich disability community histories remain unexplored; and so on. Schools, like the society that houses them, reflect an array of biases and beliefs about normalcy and worthiness that communicate a lack of belonging to many students. When schools use exclusionary discipline, those biases surface.[29]

Exclusionary discipline, which involves removing students from the classroom through punishments such as suspensions and expulsions, dramatically increased in the United States over several decades as a result of zero-tolerance policies that use such approaches even for the most minor offenses, including nonviolent "misbehavior," such as tardiness, talking, texting, or sleeping in class, or subjective behaviors, such as "willful defiance" or "disrespect,"[30] with little consideration of the context and underlying causes of these behaviors.

In 2017–2018, nearly 5% of all K–12 students received at least one out-of-school suspension, but the rates were more than twice as high (12%) for Black students and were also disproportionately high for Native students (7%) and for students with disabilities (9%).[31] (See Table 4.1.) This is not because students of color misbehave more but because they receive significantly more disciplinary consequences, including harsher and longer punishments than White students for the same disciplinable offenses, as well as for behavior that isn't actually offensive.[32] The U.S. Department of Education has also reported that "a consistent pattern persists of schools suspending or expelling black students with disabilities at higher rates than their proportion of the population of students with disabilities" since data collection began in 1998–1999.[33] In 2017–2018, CRDC data show that:

Table 4.1. Proportion of Students Who Received One or More Out-of-School Suspensions, by Race/Ethnicity, Disability Status, and English Learner Status (2017-2018)

Student Group	Out of School Suspension Rates
Asian	1.0%
Black	12.1%
Hawaiian/ Pacific Islander	4.8%
Latinx	3.8%
Native American	6.8%
Two or More Races	5.4%
White	3.3%
Students with disabilities	9.3%
Students without disabilities	4.1%
English learners	3.5%
Non-English learners	4.9%
Male	6.6%
Female	2.9%

Source: LPI analysis of U.S. Department of Education, Office for Civil Rights, Civil Rights Data Collection, 2017–2018, from Leung, M., Scott, C., Losen, D., & Campoli, A. (2022). *Inequitable opportunity to learn: Out of school suspensions.* Learning Policy Institute.

- Black students with disabilities made up 2.3% of the student population but were 8.8% of students receiving one or more out-of-school suspensions.
- Students with disabilities made up 13.2% of the enrolled student population, but 38.1% of expulsions.
- Black students comprised 15.1% of enrollments, but 33.3% of expulsions without educational services. Black girls were suspended at rates almost double their enrollment and Black boys were suspended at rates more than triple their enrollment.
- These trends were even more severe in preschool, where Black students accounted for 18.2% of total preschool enrollment but received 43.3% of out-of-school suspensions, and preschool students with identified disabilities accounted for 22.7% of total preschool enrollment but accounted for 56.9% of expulsions.[34]

Observational research has shown that this may be a function, in part, of implicit bias among teachers. For example, in an eye-tracking study, teachers were asked to watch six minutes of video content of young children playing and scan for any "problem behaviors." Although there were no problem behaviors present, teachers focused significantly more of their attention on Black children, and on Black boys in particular.[35] In a number of laboratory experiments and field studies, researchers have found that this kind of biased expectation of Black children appears among teachers, college students, and police officers: when experimenters invoke concepts of trouble, crime, or delinquency, participants are more likely to direct their eye gaze toward Black faces, as opposed to White faces, even when the Black face is that of a young boy.[36]

In all, students missed 11,205,797 school days due to out-of-school suspensions during the 2017–2018 academic year.[37] Any lost time is a challenge for learning. By one estimate, during the 2015–2016 school year, nationally, Black students lost 66 days of instructional time per 100 students, five times that lost by White students, and Black students with disabilities lost approximately 77 more days (per 100 enrolled) than White students with disabilities.[38] A study estimating the time that students and administrators could reclaim by investing in measures to reduce punitive discipline and exclusion found that a middle school recovered the equivalent of 82 eight-hour days by undertaking a more positive approach to discipline.[39]

The personal, academic, and life-shaping consequences of exclusions from school can be profound. They include:

- lost learning time;[40]
- lost sense of belonging and engagement in school;[41]
- significantly increased likelihood of school dropout;[42] and
- significantly increased risk of future incarceration.[43]

A Texas study found that suspended or expelled students were almost three times more likely to have contact with the juvenile criminal punishment system the following year,[44] and national Civil Rights Data Collection (CRDC) data collected by the Office for Civil Rights for 2017–2018 showed that Black students were disproportionately represented among those referred to law enforcement (28.7%) or arrested at school (31.6%), while they constituted only 15.1% of the student population. Similarly, Black students with identified disabilities (2.3% of enrolled students) made up 8.4% of those referred to law enforcement and 9.1% of those arrested.[45]

School suspension and other exclusionary practices produce neither behavioral nor academic benefits;[46] they are also associated with *decreases* in academic achievement and test scores.[47] When students feel unwelcome at school, it affects their motivation. Lost time in the classroom and missed assignments are difficult to recoup, and students quickly fall behind. Furthermore, students notice disparities in the application of discipline, so when they belong to a targeted group, their sense of belonging falters, and they become less engaged academically.[48]

Exclusionary discipline also has a negative impact on school climate, which is so important to achievement, as well as on ratings of school governance, as significant time needed for learning, community-building, and staff development is instead spent tending to disciplinary concerns.[49] The lack of attention to staff development in many schools focused on punitive discipline can create a vicious cycle, since research finds that less-prepared teachers, who would most benefit from staff development on productive teaching strategies, tend to exclude students more.[50]

RESTORATIVE PRACTICES

A growing number of schools have sought to replace exclusionary discipline policies with a set of schoolwide *restorative practices*, which "proactively build healthy relationships and a sense of community to prevent and address conflict and wrongdoing."[51] Restorative practices create caring school relationships (instead of reward-and-punishment schemes for behavior management) by infusing SEL and community-building activities into the school day through community circles and other processes for sharing events and feelings and by accessing supports when they are needed. In addition, they allow students to reflect on their behavior and make amends when needed to preserve the health of the community, rather than be pushed out of school.[52] These practices support deeper learning, as students learn to reflect on their feelings and actions, develop empathy and interpersonal skills, and engage in increasingly sophisticated problem-solving within their school communities.

Restorative Practices at Bronxdale High School

Bronxdale High School is an inclusion high school serving 445 students, about one quarter of whom are students with disabilities, in a low-income community of color in New York City. The once chaotic and unsafe site is now a safe, caring, and collaborative community in which staff, students, and families have voice, agency, and responsibility, and in which students are graduating and going on to college at rates higher than their peers across the city. At Bronxdale, community-building—accomplished through social and emotional learning work in advisories, student-designed classroom constitutions, and supportive affirmations and community development in all classrooms—is integral to the now-successful restorative approach.

As Principal Carolyne Quintana described, restorative practices have value only when there is something to restore, and that something is "the community, relationships, and harmony." As one student commented, "We're connected. Students and teachers care about you." Still another stated, "Every student in this school has at least one relationship with a teacher." Much of the foundational work is done in advisory classes, which are led by teachers and other professional staff and supported by student leaders in the school, who receive training to do so. By creating public spaces for students to make their coping strategies explicit, advisories create opportunities for members of a community to share knowledge and skills in support of each other.

At Bronxdale, the restorative approach is not a behavior management system to keep the school and students under control, although it does have the effect of creating a safe, respectful environment. Rather, it is a student development strategy that helps students develop prosocial ways of responding to the stresses and tensions that affect them in their daily lives and that will serve them well in forging successful, productive, and satisfying lives going forward. In that sense, the approach is both educative (focused on creating positive norms and teaching useful strategies) and restorative (able to help repair problems or harms).

Restorative practices aim to establish and sustain relationships, harmony, and the sense of community that are a precursor to community members' understanding that violating community norms harms their community. Staff want students to understand the importance of taking conscious action to repair the harm done in order to restore the community's integrity, harmony, and relationships, as well as their membership in it. Punitive approaches might generate individual remorse for harm done, but punishment does not teach students the value of community and community membership or the consequences of community lost. This is why Quintana advises other principals who ask about restorative programs for their schools to start not by importing a program, but by building a community, after which a variety of programs can be helpful.

Restorative deans—staff assigned full-time to support the building of community and implementation of a restorative justice approach—work with other staff and with students directly to teach students behavioral skills and responsibility, and repair harm by making amends through restorative practices such as peer mediation, circles, and youth court. The restorative deans' work is also supported by teachers, social workers, counselors, and community partners who are part of the school's multitiered system of support (MTSS) that enables trauma-informed and healing-informed supports for students. As one of these deans put it, the school's goal is "getting students not to respond to their tensions in a violent way anywhere." A student explained that at Bronxdale, "You get a chance to fix what you did. They don't suspend you." Another remarked, "Here we learn about consequences. In other schools, we would get punished for everything."

At the core of Bronxdale's conception of the restorative approach are the staff's positive beliefs about and their faith in the fundamental worthiness of students. This sentiment is crystalized by Deans Flores and Restrepo, who express the view that although kids sometimes have problems, they are not themselves the problem. They explain that their goal is to help staff shift to the idea that "kids do what they can. If they can't, it's because they don't know how." The deans reject the idea that the students are defective and in need of character fixing or punishment; instead, they assert the belief that creating school as a caring community can, itself, elicit more prosocial behaviors from students. By helping students understand that they have choices in their responses and can think in new ways, which will give them choices, the staff supports students in imagining, learning, and adopting such behaviors.

Source: Adapted from Ancess, J., Rogers, B., Duncan Grand, D., & Darling- Hammond, L. (2019). *Teaching the way students learn best: Lessons from Bronxdale High School.* Learning Policy Institute.

The restorative practices in use at Bronxdale High School work together with a project-based curriculum that engages students in motivating inquiries and culminates in "passion projects" that allow seniors to dive deeply into research on a topic of their choice, which they examine and present in an exhibition to other students and teachers, often creating a new product that represents their learning. Motivation to attend school and to support the community is reinforced by the nature of the learning process as well as by the supportive environment they encounter.

A number of alternatives to exclusionary discipline have been tried at scale and found productive when implemented well. Such efforts as Positive Behavior Intervention and Support,[53] restorative justice,[54] SEL,[55] and ecological approaches to classroom management[56] have demonstrated positive behavioral and academic outcomes, including:

- decreased exclusionary discipline; lost instructional time; disparities in disciplinary action by race and socioeconomic status; misbehavior and violence; dropout rates;
- increased prosocial behavior; student connectedness to school; attendance; test scores; academic performance; grades; graduation rates; parent engagement; parent–child communication; and
- improved teacher and student assessments of school climate, safety, opportunity, and leadership.

Many researchers note that the power of these efforts to disrupt the school-to-prison pipeline is in their attention to improving the environments that struggling students are in rather than placing the onus on students. Resources and practices like counseling, alternative work spaces (private, quiet), and restorative practices are among the many that practitioners can provide to support prosocial behavior and problem-solving within a community of care.[57]

COMMUNITY SCHOOLS AND WRAPAROUND SUPPORTS

The restorative and supportive practices described above should ideally be nested within a whole-child approach that attends to children's needs more broadly and designs all facets of the school—from school structures to curriculum to teaching practices.[58] In a school designed for whole child equity, such as a full-service community school, students have access to nutritious food, health care, and social supports; strong relationships; educative and restorative disciplinary practices; and deeper learning opportunities that are designed to activate and engage them while supporting their motivation and self-confidence to persevere and succeed. Such resources are especially important when students are grappling with poverty and toxic stress. As the U.S. Department of Education's Equity Commission noted:

> Healthier students are better learners. Strategically planned and evidence-based school health programs and services have been shown to have a positive correlation with academic achievement. Taking thoughtful steps to make school-based health services accessible to high-poverty schools and districts and to remote schools and districts can result in healthier students, better educational achievement, and lasting long-term physical and socioeconomic benefits.[59]

Designing for overall well-being makes it possible for children to learn in deep, meaningful, and lasting ways. Community schools offer a purposeful design and an evidence-based approach to advance whole-child education by offering integrated supports for physical and mental health, as well as social services of many kinds; expanded and enriched learning time before and after school and in the summer, as well as community connections to project-based work in the classroom; family and community engagement through home visits, parent–student–teacher conferencing, and regular communication with classroom teachers or advisors; and collaborative leadership and practices that engage staff, families, and community organizations in a common understanding of child development that guides joint efforts. Together, these features have been found to support stronger attendance, achievement, and attainment in high need communities.[60] As the description of Oakland International High School (below) illustrates, the provision of these resources can make an enormous difference in the capacity of students to survive and thrive.

OAKLAND INTERNATIONAL HIGH SCHOOL: A COMMUNITY SCHOOL IN ACTION

Colorful murals decorate the entrance to Oakland International High School, welcoming students, staff, and visitors to this small-by-design community school in the Oakland Unified School District (OUSD). Tucked away on a quiet street of a busy Oakland neighborhood, the school is a sanctuary for its nearly 400 students, all of whom are recently arrived immigrants. As part of the Internationals Network, Oakland International combines a commitment to rigorous academics, linguistic dignity, and bilingualism with a high-touch community school infrastructure. The result is a school that excels at preparing students for their new lives in the United States.

Students at Oakland International represent 27 countries and more than 30 languages. Some are refugees escaping conflict in their home countries, and many arrive with gaps in their education experience. In 2019, more than onethird of students were unaccompanied minors. All are English learners. Although staff recognize students' difficult histories and challenging circumstances, they also celebrate and tap into students' unique assets. As Learning Lab Co-Director Lauren Markham explains, "We can make a list all day long of the challenges students bring into the classrooms and what struggles they might have, but we want to turn the lens to the assets and strengths that they're bringing."

Oakland International's high-touch community school model provides the relational glue and comprehensive supports that are key to student success. In 2019, 93% of its students graduated within 5 years, well above state and local graduation rates, and 59% had passed the rigorous courses required for admission to California state universities. By comparison, English learners in OUSD had a graduation rate of only 62% and newcomers had an even lower graduation rate of 42%. Just 21% of newcomers districtwide graduated with the courses required for admission to a state university.

Just as importantly, Oakland International students feel motivated, empowered, and connected to the school and the larger community. As one student shares, "The school has helped me a lot in preparing me to go to college. They connected me to many programs outside the school, like internships or volunteer programs, which have prepared me to go to college with experience being a leader and [knowing] how to use my voice."

As a community school, Oakland International is well positioned to build relationships with students and families and to connect them to a broad array of programs, services, and supports by leveraging partnerships: An onsite Wellness Center functions like a one-stop shop for students to access a variety of supports, from emergency housing and food to legal assistance or mental health services. For medical, counseling, and health education services, Oakland International partners with Oakland Technical High School (Oakland Tech), just five blocks away. Students from both schools are served by TechniClinic, a health clinic located on the Oakland Tech campus. Managed by La Clínica de la Raza, TechniClinic is one of OUSD's school-based health centers, a districtwide approach to addressing disparities in education, health, and life outcomes for students. Through the partnership, students from Oakland International—many of whom do not have medical insurance— have access to free and confidential health care, removing a common barrier to regular school attendance.

During the COVID-19 pandemic, the school:

- Created an interactive virtual school portal to serve as a dynamic way for students to access what they needed for virtual learning and other supports;

- Activated a system of checking in with students and providing tutoring support by identifying additional adults—besides classroom teachers—who could work with students outside of traditional school hours so they did not fall behind;
- Raised more than $100,000 to distribute to students and families for housing, food, and other basic needs;
- Assisted with the paperwork required to file for unemployment or apply for direct government support; and
- Held a weekly food pickup on-site and delivered 70 food boxes per week to families.

Since then, the school has adjusted and expanded programs to meet the needs and realities of their students' lives. Internships are being redesigned, for example, to allow for paid employment. The school is also expanding its career and technical education support and is planning to offer classes on Saturdays and during other nonstandard hours in an effort to recognize and support students who must work to provide for themselves and their families.

Oakland International cultivates a learning community that supports the academic success of its students both during the traditional school day, through project-based learning, and after school, through sports and other enrichment programs. Peer tutors and "newcomer assistants" (staff members who provide individualized support and tutoring after school and on the weekends) add another layer of support. Classes at Oakland International combine warmly supportive practices and rigorous academics in classrooms organized around collaborative projects that integrate English learning with academic content that connects to students' lives, communities, and current events.

Powerful academic growth, language acquisition, and social–emotional development also occur outside of the regular school day. A partnership with Soccer Without Borders provides after-school programming that marries soccer with community-building and academic and language supports. The model reflects Oakland International's belief that language learning happens all the time. And most importantly for many students, the program connects them to a supportive community in which youth from different countries who speak different languages are able to connect and bond over the universal language of soccer.

Oakland International employs a variety of strategies to engage and support families, including English as a second language classes (many parents of Oakland International students are also English learners), a communal garden and cooking classes, a legal services clinic, and college and career information nights. All of the services and supports for families are grounded in a commitment to building respectful and trusting relationships. Surveys and focus groups provide an ongoing mechanism to solicit input from parents and caregivers, as do informal gatherings like a monthly "Coffee With Counselors."

Two practices—home visits and community walks—take teachers and staff into the homes and neighborhoods of their students and families. During community walks, which are designed and led by students and families, teachers are introduced to important neighborhood landmarks and cultural centers and meet with community leaders. Walks also provide an opportunity for school staff to meet with families in their homes or another community gathering place to discuss families' questions, concerns, and hopes for their students and the school. Because Oakland International students come from many diverse backgrounds, cultures, and experiences, these walks play an important role in the development of trusting relationships and in the undoing of implicit bias. The walks also flip the script on who is teaching and who is learning: Teachers become the students, and students and families become the teachers, sharing their expertise, resources, and assets.

Source: Adapted from Hu, A. *Supporting newcomers through a community school model.* Learning Policy Institute. https://learningpolicyinstitute.org/blog/supporting-newcomers-through-community-school-model

THE CIVIL RIGHTS CONTRIBUTION AND ROAD AHEAD

There are several ways that civil rights enforcement and associated investments in educational programs have made—and continue to make—a significant difference in securing positive and inclusive school environments. Because federal civil rights law requires that schools receiving federal funding ensure that policies and procedures—including those that guide discipline—are not discriminatory, the U.S. Department of Education's Office for Civil Rights (OCR) has standing to monitor suspension and expulsion rates and bring actions in districts that have large and disproportionate rates of exclusion. This monitoring is accomplished through the Civil Rights Data Collection, which illustrates the kinds of disparities documented earlier in this chapter. During the Obama administration, many actions were brought where there was evidence of discriminatory exclusion from school, and remedies were proposed and implemented to secure more productive, inclusive responses.

Significant redress was stimulated by the Department of Education's finding that disproportionate suspensions of students with disabilities, which are even more disproportionate when race is factored in,[61] are violations of the 14th Amendment's equal protection requirements for public education and of Title VI of the Civil Rights Act, which prohibits discrimination in any federally funded activity. Such exclusions also violate the Americans With Disabilities Act (ADA), which Congress enacted in 1990 to establish a "national mandate" for eliminating discrimination against people with disabilities and to "invoke the sweep of congressional authority, including the power to enforce the

Fourteenth Amendment . . . in order to address the major areas of discrimination faced day-to-day by people with disabilities."[62] Under the ADA, a student cannot be excluded from participation in or be denied the benefits of such schools on the basis of disability.

Based on the set of civil rights laws that bear on these issues, the U.S. Department of Education and the U.S. Department of Justice launched a collaborative project in 2011 called the Supportive School Discipline Initiative, to end discriminatory discipline and to "support the use of school discipline practices that foster safe, supportive, and productive learning environments while keeping students in school."[63] The agencies issued joint guidance in January 2014 to assist public schools in meeting their obligations under federal law to administer student discipline without discriminating on the basis of race, color, or national origin.[64]

The departments issued additional guidance regarding students with disabilities that not only documented the negative effects of discriminatory discipline, but also drew on research illustrating how schools can develop SEL programs, restorative practices, and positive school climates to offer alternatives to exclusionary discipline practices and to create healthier, safer environments for all students. It was useful both in educating districts and in seeking appropriate remedies in districts that were violating students' civil rights through discipline policies. Unfortunately, this guidance was repealed by the Trump administration, and civil rights enforcement in this area slowed. However, many states and districts had already begun to reshape their discipline policies in more restorative directions, and the guidance is being reinstated by the Biden administration, along with technical assistance to districts that are looking for more productive solutions.

ESSA includes investments under Titles I and IV for programs that can support SEL,[65] restorative practices,[66] and positive school climate development. Funding for these supports was increased in the budget bills passed in 2019 and 2020. Furthermore, ESSA requires that states collect and monitor data that aid in tracking disparate impact, including "rates of in-school and out-of-school suspensions, expulsions, school-related arrests, referrals to law enforcement, and incidences of school violence (including bullying and harassment)."[67]

States are now allowed to choose indicators for their accountability systems that encourage inclusivity, like school climate (measured through student surveys), and measures of suspension and school absences, among others. The goal is to stimulate state support and local practice to create welcoming school environments, which also improve safety, behavior, and learning.[68] As of this writing, nine states include a measure of suspension in their statewide accountability and improvement systems, either for school identification or improvement purposes, in schools identified for support and intervention. Three of these states also include a student expulsion measure for improvement purposes. An additional 20 states and Washington, DC describe in their state plans how they are using suspension rate information within their broader systems to inform continuous school improvement across all schools.[69]

The focus brought to these issues by OCR under the Obama administration has had wide-reaching effects beyond the federal government's own policies. For example, at the state level, zero-tolerance legislation has stalled or been repealed in recent years. Whereas about seven bills expanding suspension or expulsion have been enacted in state legislatures in the past 5 years, in that same time frame, state legislatures enacted at least 36 bills restricting the use of suspension or expulsion or encouraging the use of alternative school discipline strategies—demonstrating a movement away from zerotolerance and toward lesspunitive strategies. Generally, these bills place limitations on the length of suspension or expulsion, disallow the use of suspension or expulsion in the early grades, require consideration of student circumstances and context, and/or encourage the use of alternative strategies.[70] When states approach the creation of a positive, inclusive climate holistically—using all of the legislative, regulatory, and financial tools at their disposal—substantial benefits for student learning are possible, as the case of California illustrates.

CALIFORNIA'S HOLISTIC APPROACH TO CREATING SAFE AND INCLUSIVE SCHOOLS

California began its effort to reduce the use of exclusionary discipline and create safe and inclusive environments for children when the state passed a new Local Control Funding Formula in 2013, which changed how schools are governed and funded, and set eight state priorities to govern accountability and continuous improvement at the state and local level. Among these priorities is school climate, which districts must evaluate with student surveys every two years and report on as part of the Local Control Accountability Plan. California also includes suspension rates in its statewide school accountability system under the Every Student Succeeds Act, tracking progress and status on this indicator annually and using the results to inform the public and to determine schools eligible for support and intervention.

To reduce the use of exclusionary practices, the state repealed its zero-tolerance policies and replaced them with policies that encourage restorative practices. The California Department of Education (CDE) also took legislative action after the data revealed that certain subgroups of students experienced a disproportionate percentage of expulsions and suspensions for nonviolent behaviors, such as willful defiance. In 2013, California lawmakers passed Assembly Bill 420, limiting suspensions and expulsions for disruptive behavior in grades K-3, and in 2020 the ban was expanded to grades 4-8 as well. To support these efforts, the California Commission on Teacher Credentialing passed new initial licensing standards for teachers and administrators, including competencies in teaching social–emotional skills and in using restorative practices. In addition, the state has funded professional development focused on helping educators develop social-emotional supports for students, as well as restorative justice practices centered on promoting respect, taking responsibility, and strengthening relationships. The California Department of Education has initiated forums and workshops to make districts, administrators, and teachers aware of successful alternatives to suspensions and expulsions and to support more constructive approaches.

As a result of these approaches, California has achieved a sharp decrease in suspension rates while making schools safer. Between 2011 and 2016, suspensions declined by 33.6%, driven by a 77% decline in suspensions for "willful defiance," and expulsions dropped by 40.4%. According to national data, school-based firearm incidents in the state, which were well above the national average in 2009–2010, were far below the national average by 2015–2016, declining by more than 50% in the 7-year period. Significant decreases also occurred in rates of school-based fights, bullying incidents, and classroom disruptions over that period.

Since the 2011–2012 academic year, California has had sharp declines in suspensions and expulsions overall and in comparison to other states. According to the Civil Rights Data Collection, by 2017–2018, the state's out-of-school-suspension rate had dropped to 4.9%, one of the lowest rates in the country. By 2019–2020, state data show suspensions had dropped further, to 3.5%. Researchers found that these declines have held true for all racial and socioeconomic groups and school levels, narrowing disciplinary gaps among racial and ethnic groups across the state. High school graduation rates, reaching 84% by 2020, have also increased in California since 2010, when they were 74%.

Continuing its approach to wrapping students with needed supports, the 2021 budget included an additional $4 billion for mental health services for youth, $3 billion for full-service community schools across the state, nearly $2 billion for expanded learning programs (after school and summer school), and full funding for universal meals.

Source: Adapted from Cardichon, J., & Darling-Hammond, L. (2019). *Protecting students' civil rights: The federal role in school discipline,* pp. 10–11. Learning Policy Institute, and updated with more recent data, including California's Budget Act for 2020–21. https://www.cde.ca .gov/fg/fr/eb/yr20ltr0929.asp

At the federal level, modest funding has been included for many years for Safe and Healthy schools and for community schools initiatives, which support providing integrated services for young people through ESSA's Title IV. These range from health and mental health programming to counseling and social work. The 2022 federal budget expanded funding for full-service community school models, and the American Rescue Plan Act, which provided $130 billion for K–12 schools, allowed for investments in social–emotional and mental health supports, nutrition supports, and community schools' expansion. These investments help establish a pathway to healthy development on which other educational elements can build.

The shift from exclusionary zero tolerance policies to those supporting students to stay in schools would not have occurred without the civil rights activism and enforcement that establishes students' rights to equitable access to an inclusive environment. Next steps along this road include:

- Continued vigilance from the Office of Civil Rights to address disciplinary disparities that come to light through the Civil Rights Data Collection and complaints, and the reissuance of guidance for ending exclusionary discipline and infusing restorative practices in their stead;
- Expansion of federally sanctioned opportunities to enable states to incorporate indicators of safe and inclusive climates and other student supports in their systems of accountability and continuous improvement, as signaled in recent Department of Education guidance; and
- Continued, stable, and expanded investments in federal and state programs promoting social–emotional learning, restorative practices, physical and mental health supports, and full-service community schools, including federal partnerships with states to create systemic initiatives, so that these essentials become the norm and are viewed as part of a right to supportive education, instead of the exception for students' learning environments.

In addition to these moves, we will need to acknowledge in professional preparation systems that providing such educational experiences calls for a high level of sophistication and skill from adults, who must understand not only how child development progresses over time, but also that it can be dynamic—showing up differently in response to particular contexts and experiences. These adults must also become experts at managing their emotions and communicating effectively. We turn in the next chapter to the means for securing an expert staff that can provide the kind of high-quality teaching that is essential for all other efforts to succeed.

CHAPTER 5

High-Quality Teaching

The experience of [high-performing] school systems suggests that three things matter most: 1) getting the right people to become teachers; 2) developing them into effective instructors; and 3) ensuring that the system is able to deliver the best possible instruction for every child.

—Michael Barber and Mona Mourshed,
How the World's Best-Performing School Systems Come Out on Top[1]

The importance of teachers cannot be overstated. As the primary arbiters of students' daily school-based experiences, they, along with principals, hold tremendous power to construct the learning environment and, indeed, to define what learning is. On the road to deeper learning there must be teachers who are trained to deliver innovative curriculum using inclusive, dynamic pedagogy and who believe that all children can, and deserve to, learn. These teachers deserve support, livable wages, and affirmation—and if they are to be present in all classrooms and communities, these conditions must be made commonplace. As noted earlier, a well-resourced system, coupled with a whole-child approach, creates the ecosystem in which teaching for deeper learning and equity can grow and flourish.

TEACHING FOR DEEPER LEARNING

Classrooms in which deeper learning is the goal are ones where meaningful academic content is paired with engaging, experiential, and innovative learning experiences. Such experiences equip students with the skills to find, analyze, and apply knowledge in new and emerging contexts and prepare them for college, work, civic participation, and lifelong learning in a fast-changing and information-rich world. These kinds of experiences—and the teachers who can provide them—are often inequitably reserved for students in affluent communities, private schools, advanced classes, or "gifted" or honors tracks within heterogeneous schools.

Teaching for deeper learning requires a much more extensive repertoire of skills and practices than teaching for superficial coverage of content. Teaching complex skills to students with diverse learning needs requires sophisticated pedagogy. Research on teachers who teach diverse students effectively finds that they support learning by:

- creating ambitious and meaningful tasks that reflect how knowledge is used in the field;
- engaging students in active learning so that they apply and test what they know;
- drawing connections to students' prior knowledge and experiences;
- diagnosing student understanding to scaffold the learning process step by step;
- assessing student learning continuously and adapting teaching to student needs;
- providing clear standards, constant feedback, and opportunities for revising work; and
- encouraging strategic and metacognitive thinking so that students can learn to evaluate and guide their own learning.[2]

Teaching that aims at deep learning, rather than merely coverage of material, requires well-informed judgments about what and how different students are learning, what gaps in their understanding need to be addressed, what experiences will allow them to connect what they know to what they need and want to know, and what instructional adaptations will be needed to ensure that they can reach common goals. In fact, the more common the expectations for achievement are across a wide range of students, the more variable must be the teaching strategies for reaching these goals. If teaching is uniform, assuming a single mode and pace of learning, learners who start at different places and learn in different ways will end with greatly unequal achievement. To accomplish equity, teachers must be able to personalize the learning experience, supporting different modalities for learning and individualizing supports to meet student needs.

These pedagogies are typically the product of teacher preparation rooted in knowledge about child development and learning as these occur in cultural contexts; supportive of skills for developing identity-safe, affirming classrooms in which all students claim membership; focused on designing authentic, engaging curriculum and assessments; and attentive to children's learning. This kind of preparation offers extended clinical experiences in schools and classrooms where these practices already operate, tightly connected to relevant coursework that also models deeper learning for candidates.[3]

We saw this kind of teaching in Ted Pollen's classroom at Midtown West in New York City (see Chapter 1), a school that is staffed largely by Bank Street College graduates who are well-prepared and student-centered. As a Black teacher in a diverse school setting, Ted also provides role modeling, cultural perspective, and affirmation for his students that can be enabling. As we describe later in this chapter, the city's ability to attract and retain teachers like Ted has relied in substantial part on civil rights litigation over a number of years.

Preparation

Around the country, the ability to develop teachers like Ted depends on high-quality preparation programs that enable teachers to learn the sophisticated skills of teaching challenging content to students who learn in different ways—and that are affordable for diverse teachers to undertake when they are entering a profession that pays less than others. Teacher residency models—which are university–school district partnerships that combine top-flight clinical training with applied coursework, and support residents financially in exchange for a teaching commitment of 3 to 5 years—are demonstrating considerable success in preparing a diverse cadre of effective teachers who enter and stay in high-need schools.[4]

A study of one such program—the San Francisco Teacher Residency (SFTR), which partnered with the Stanford Teacher Education Program and the University of San Francisco—illustrates how strong preparation helps teachers to skillfully design and manage inquiry-based teaching that not only promotes deep understanding of the concepts being learned, but also opens pathways into the material that meet the needs of diverse learners.

Because learners are building on different kinds of prior knowledge and have distinctive ways of accessing and processing information, they require different kinds of scaffolds and reinforcements. In the lesson described below, a resident from the Stanford Teacher Education Program illustrates the use of a wide range of pedagogical and curriculum-building skills in working with an inclusion class of high school students—half of them identified for special education—in a high-poverty school. Drawing on what she has learned in her Curriculum and Instruction course about unit planning, we can see how she supports guided inquiry, checking for understanding and adapting instruction as needed, providing multiple ways to access the course content, and differentiating instruction.

LEARNING TO TEACH FOR DEEPER LEARNING

On a sunny March day at June Jordan School for Equity in San Francisco, Jody DeAraujo—a teacher resident in the San Francisco Teacher Residency—teaches a lesson about the effects of pH on an ecosystem to a diverse group of 9th- and 10th-graders in a block period field biology class. Eight of the 16 students in the class today are identified for special education and have individualized education plans.

Jody's lesson centers on teaching the concept of pH through a real-world example of how CO_2 combines with H_2O in the ocean to make the water more acidic, thus lowering the pH value. Class begins with a whole-class warm-up activity. Jody reviews a range-of-tolerance graph that had been shared in the previous lesson. She asks, "What would happen to the ecosystem if the pH changed from 7 to 6?" Students share responses, and she asks "What would happen if the pH changed? What's actually happening in the real world?" A student responds, "Global warming."

The next part of this fast-paced lesson involves students working in pairs through a set of questions on ocean acidification to understand how and why pH in the ocean is changing. Jody intentionally pairs up the students and provides them with two images—which she reminds them are similar to the graphs they will have on an upcoming quiz. One is a time series graph of CO_2 levels in the North Pacific and the ocean pH between 1958 and 2012, and the other is a picture depicting how atmospheric carbon dioxide and water create carbonic acid. The students get to work in their pairs, spending the next 15 minutes deciphering the images in front of them and answering a set of questions Jody has given them about ocean acidification. Jody and her cooperating teacher (CT), Lenore Kenny, circulate around the classroom supporting pairs who need it and redirecting a couple of distracted students.

Jody then leads the class through a series of short activities designed to deepen students' understanding of ocean acidification and provide different entry points for students still struggling with the concept. First, Jody screens a 5-minute video on ocean acidification, after which she questions the class to assess their understanding. Next, students work in pairs to read and annotate two short texts (one on ocean acidification and another on coral reefs), and then complete the response questions. Then Jody leads the class through a post-reading no-stakes check-in quiz to check their understanding.

The last 30 minutes of the class are led by the cooperating teacher, who works with the students on their Ecosystem Data Collection project, a 2-week project they are undertaking. Jody has solo responsibility for a class period she teaches later in the day. However, in this period, she and her CT operate on a co-teaching model. Her CT, Lenore, will often model a lesson when teaching with Jody in the co-teaching model, which Jody will then teach on her own the following day during her solo period. The staggered lessons allow Jody to maximize the benefit of Lenore's modeling, reflecting on what she has seen and done and then adapting it based on her own style.

Lenore asks students to take out their observation sheets for their ecosystem project. Each group of students has a container with two fish (their ecosystem), which they have designed themselves. Lenore asks students to observe the fish and use clues to determine why their fish are or are not still alive. Students are very engaged in observing their fish and figuring out whether and why their fish have died. Lenore says, "I want you to write detailed observations. At this point, there are detailed changes happening. How many people have seen *Law and Order*? They're trying to figure out by looking at clues: Why is it dead?" She then points out that a student named Christian has said something that the rest should all hear. She says, "Sometimes you can add up all the clues and there's not a good reason you can see. Sometimes the fish just dies of something that led to its demise, its death. You have 15 minutes. You should be writing that whole time."

The students come back together after 15 minutes. Lenore asks students to read their observations out loud. She calls on one student: "Alan, read me one of your observations. Out loud so everyone can hear."

Alan responds, "I see the fishes are dead and they're floating and their eyes are white."

She probes, "Was there anything in the water around them? Was there another fish chewing on them? Or are they all dead? What did their tails and their fins look like? I want to give people a sense of how thorough I want you to be. Give me another one."

Another student says, "The plants are growing."

"What's your evidence?"

"They're stuck on the top of the bottle," the student replies.

Lenore continues her questioning, and the student answers, describing his methods for gathering evidence. "How much did they grow?"

"Three inches."

"Did you measure it or guess?"

"Yes, I measured them."

"With a ruler? How did you know how much to measure them from the last time?"

The student replies, "Last time, they were two inches."

Lenore asks, "From the top of the soil or the bottom of the soil?," then makes a comment to the whole class, which explains the reason for her close questioning: "Is everyone understanding the depth of the observations?" She asks for one more example. "Give me one reason why your fish might have died. The tube that they have is in the water."

She waits a moment, then adds, "One end of the tube is in the water. The other side is where the plants are at. So the fish are swimming in CO_2. There wasn't enough CO_2 going into the top. When Ms. DeAraujo was teaching, you learned we're polluting the air with a lot of CO_2. Maybe some CO_2 is getting from the animal into the water." She then sends the students back to their ecosystems to do a more thorough analysis, reminding them to measure the plants and to look at the fish fins and gills.

Following the lesson, Jody and her collaborating teacher debrief the lesson, reflecting as colleagues on whether their objectives had been achieved, whether they had reached all students, and whether the lesson had engaged the students in deeper learning. The collaborative relationship between Jody and Lenore, and their mutual work in teaching, is evident. Additionally, it is clear that the resident is both a teacher and a learner in this activity— having the opportunity, like her students, to apply what she is learning in practice rather than only in theory. Jody independently led the first part of the lesson, but then had the opportunity to observe her CT modeling inquiry practices—pushing students on their observations of the ecosystem they have built, getting them to be specific and descriptive and to provide evidence for their conclusions.

This final part of the class period is part of a larger 2-week-long project involving building, observing, and developing hypotheses about an ecosystem, and testing those hypotheses. The project provided an opportunity for students to learn academic content—the factors that influence an ecosystem—while building their scientific analysis and writing skills, collaborating with a partner, and persevering through this extended project.

Jody had the opportunity to collaborate with her CT on the design of this project, observe her CT leading this project, and then lead it herself in the solo class she teaches each day—having collaborated with Lenore in teaching the same content earlier. Jody also reflected on how her lesson was informed by her Science Curriculum and Instruction course at Stanford. In the activity in which she had students look at the CO_2 ocean acidification graph, she noted:

> The questions were very much like guided inquiry. That's definitely something I learned a lot from my Curriculum and Instruction teacher at Stanford. He's fantastic. One thing I learned is to use "confirmatory reading." You don't want to introduce language to students through a reading. The reading should be the last step. So that's why I had them to do the readings right at the end after we had three lessons on pH and ocean acidification and range of tolerance. I felt like now we can do a reading and really confirm what you know. These words aren't going to be new to you.

Jody added that she uses formative assessments to check for students' understanding of the material. In this class, for example, she did the formative assessment after a series of learning activities that helped her learn that some of her students were confused about pH increasing and decreasing. Jody included the video in her lesson to support multiple access points for student understanding, something that she and her classmates had talked about in their coursework. Because readings are not equally accessible for all students, she used a few different sources of information. Likewise, to support equity-centered pedagogy, Jody went around to talk to students, checking on their understanding and scaffolding her language with the aim of meeting them where they are. She noted that some students could read the graph and it made sense to them immediately, while others could not, so she needed to do more one-on-one work with them. In reflecting on the lesson, Jody was able to identify the learning of each of her students and how her teaching moves supported their gains, while also identifying the next steps she would take to strengthen the ability of each of them to move forward.

Source: Adapted from Darling-Hammond, L., & Oakes, J. (2019). Preparing teachers for deeper learning. Harvard Education Press.

The preparation Jody received that allowed her to engage in such sophisticated practice combined two key elements: First, a rigorous teacher education curriculum that addressed issues of equity, adolescent development, learning processes, content pedagogy, curriculum development, instructional and assessment strategies, and supports for English learners and students with disabilities; and, second, a set of strong clinical supports. Spending a full year in the classroom with an expert cooperating teacher, in a school designed for deeper learning and organized for the training of novice teachers, enabled her to learn a kind of practice that relatively few teachers are able to develop even later in their careers. As we describe below, learning opportunities for teachers in the United States are uneven and undersupported. A number of policy changes are needed to make rich, high-skilled preparation—and practice—more widespread.

ACCESS TO WELL-PREPARED TEACHERS

Unfortunately, outside of newly funded residency programs, it is largely the case that the teachers best able to afford this kind of preparation to teach are distributed to our schools' most affluent and well-resourced students. In schools serving large concentrations of students of color and students from low-income families, teachers are typically less well qualified, and in times of recurring teacher shortages, large numbers of these teachers are allowed to enter on emergency permits without the necessary training to provide quality instruction.[5] Data from the most recent Civil Rights Data Collection show that schools serving the largest number of students of color employ four times as many uncertified teachers and nearly twice as many inexperienced teachers as those serving the fewest.[6]

A recent study of California districts found that the most important predictor of student achievement was teacher qualifications: The more teachers on substandard credentials, the lower student achievement across groups, with the greatest negative effects on Black and Latinx students.[7] These findings are not unusual. In a major study in North Carolina,[8] economists found that student achievement gains were significantly larger when students had teachers who were experienced, were prepared and licensed before entry, and had National Board Certification—an acknowledgment of expertise closely related to teachers' abilities to teach diverse students for deeper learning. Together, these variables had more effect on student achievement gains than the effects of race and parent education combined. However, these well-prepared teachers were inequitably distributed, with the most advantaged students disproportionately receiving the most experienced and accomplished teachers.

Several factors work in concert to create these inequalities.[9] From a resource allocation standpoint, teacher salaries and working conditions (and quality of life), school site safety, opportunities for professional development, and learning resources all depend on financial investments at the state and local levels. Funding formulas that rely on local real estate taxes as a primary re-source inevitably disadvantage communities experiencing poverty. Teachers with the most experience and training tend to have more mobility and can opt to teach where the compensation is better.

Also, it is important to note that training to become a teacher—often through a master's degree program—is costly and generally unsubsidized. Thus, such training is largely accessible only to people with disposable resources. The lack of financial support for preparation makes teacher training less accessible to potential candidates of color, who carry significantly more college debt than White candidates. Their likelihood of entering and staying in teaching is reduced by the difficulty of affording college and meeting preparation requirements, and affected by their disproportionate entry through emergency pathways or alternative routes that skip student teaching and have higher attrition rates.[10]

This has produced a profession that is currently 80% White even as students of color are now a majority in public schools. Meanwhile, a growing body of research shows the benefit of teachers of color for enabling greater achievement and attainment for students of color.[11]

The lack of financial support for teacher preparation in many states, coupled with low teacher salaries (about 30% less than other college graduates earn by mid-career)[12] creates another context for inequality, as it reduces the supply of teachers, creating shortages in the highest-need schools that are typically addressed by lowering the standards for entry rather than by increasing incentives. This undermines education in at least two ways: Teachers who are better prepared are not only more effective but also more likely to stay in teaching. Teachers who enter the profession without having completed preparation are two to three times as likely to leave the profession within the first year, creating turnover that also decreases student achievement.[13]

All of this adds up to suboptimal teaching and churn in many schools located in high-poverty communities, which are disproportionately where children of color live and are schooled. Teachers without life experience in these communities, and those who have not undertaken deep reflection on power and inequality, can reinforce damaging beliefs about children in these environments and often flee teaching quickly, forcing schools already struggling with resource shortages to find emergency staff and manage the school-level instability this causes. Turnover also has substantial financial consequences, with each teacher who leaves costing urban districts more than $20,000 to find a replacement.[15] Meanwhile, instruction under these conditions typically focuses on low-level skills organized by scripted curriculum and worksheets, buttressed by punitive discipline policies.[16]

The practice of lowering standards for entry rather than ensuring teachers have access to the knowledge they need to be effective is often excused by the argument that teaching can be learned on the job. Yet the learning curve without formal training and support is considerably steeper, which undermines efforts to build deeper learning and equity. With little knowledge to inform their decisions, teachers can draw the wrong inferences about why things went wrong and what to do about them. One underprepared recruit who entered teaching with just 6 weeks of training described how she found herself blaming her students before she left teaching after her first year to enter a teacher preparation program:

> I found myself having problems with cross-cultural teaching issues—blaming my kids because the class was crazy and out of control [and] blaming the parents as though they didn't care about their kids. It was frustrating to me to get caught up in that.

A researcher who followed a group of underprepared beginning teachers through their first year described the pathway from initial teaching failure to a rote-oriented curriculum, coupled with heavy-handed attempts at discipline based on denying students recess and other "privileges":

> That is how it begins . . . or how it begins to end. You come to your first class, and they eat you up, and you vow that it will not happen again. And you learn what you have to learn to make sure it doesn't. You learn the value of workbooks because even if they're numbingly dull, they keep the kids busy, and if the kids are busy, they are not making trouble for you.[17]

By contrast, research has found that strong teacher education enables teachers to use strategies that encourage higher-order learning and that respond to students' experiences, needs, and learning approaches.[18] Among other things, knowing how to plan and manage a classroom—including the skillful use of social–emotional community-building—allows teachers to focus on the kind of complex teaching that is needed to develop higher-order skills. Since the novel tasks required for complex problem-solving are more difficult to manage than the routine tasks associated with learning rote skills, lack of classroom management ability can lead teachers to "dumb down" the curriculum to control student work more easily.[19] Yet this kind of teaching is equally frustrating to the teachers and can contribute to the kind of high turnover seen in schools that experience shortages.

A study of the San Francisco Teacher Residency, described above, found that two-thirds of candidates were prospective teachers of color, and after 5 years, 97% of all residents were still in teaching, and 80% were still teaching in the district. This compares to only 38% of other newly hired teachers who entered the district five years earlier.[20]

In addition to investments in preparation, there is a role for professional development in increasing teachers' capacities to build trusting, safe, respectful classrooms. Such training should include understanding child and adolescent development and learning as well as how to offer "developmentally oriented instruction."[21] Effective professional development should also focus on content, incorporate active learning, support collaboration in job-embedded contexts, use modeling of effective practice, include coaching and expert support, offer opportunity for feedback and reflection, and be sustained over time.[22] Developing our teacher corps so that it can deliver effective instruction to all learners requires meaningful, consistent investments of preparation, compensation, training, collaboration, time, resources, and feedback, provided in ways that respect the need for well-being and in contexts conducive to learning and growth.[23]

THE CIVIL RIGHTS CONTRIBUTION AND ROAD AHEAD

The importance of equitable access to teachers has been acknowledged in civil rights litigation and enforcement in several ways. Over the years many lawsuits challenging school finance inequity have included claims of low access to prepared and experienced teachers for students in high-poverty schools and districts.[24] School equity cases in more than 20 states have found that by every measure of qualifications—certification, subject matter background, pedagogical training, selectivity of college attended, test scores, or experience—students of color and students from low-income families typically have the least-qualified teachers and, relatedly, the least intellectually challenging curriculum.

The *Leandro v. State of North Carolina* (1997) decision named access to qualified teachers and principals as one of the components of the educational rights to which students are entitled.[25] The decision has been followed by decades of litigation and hearings over the legislature's failure to take actions that would meet the court's ruling.[26] In 2018, the plaintiffs and defendants agreed to pursue a research-based plan.[27] Issued in 2019, the plan has been partially implemented, but major elements continue to be caught in budget disputes. The plan's elements include expansion of the state's Teaching Fellows and Principal Fellows programs, which provide funding for high-quality preparation for educators, repaid with service in the state's public schools, as well as improvements in preparation, mentoring for beginning educators, and more accessible professional development focused on deeper learning and social–emotional supports.

Court cases in several other states have also resulted in improvements in teaching. For example, Connecticut undertook a set of reforms following the 1977 *Horton v. Meskill* decision in which the Connecticut Supreme Court became one of the first of the state high courts to invalidate a state education finance system because its reliance on local property taxes generated greatly unequal spending.[28] Later reforms were prodded by the filing of the *Sheff v. O'Neill* lawsuit in 1989 that challenged racially segregated schools.[29]

Beginning in the late 1980s, Connecticut enacted some of the nation's most ambitious efforts to equalize educational opportunity by improving teaching. These reforms addressed school funding disparities by providing financial incentives to raise teachers' salaries, allocating funds to districts on an equalizing basis. This approach infused resources explicitly targeted at the improvement of teaching into low-wealth districts. The initiative was studied by the National

Education Goals Panel when the state's efforts resulted in sharp increases in student performance and reductions in achievement gaps between advantaged and disadvantaged pupils. Following steep gains throughout the decade, by 1998, 4th-graders ranked first in the nation in reading and mathematics on the National Assessment of Educational Progress (NAEP), despite increasing numbers of students from low-income families, minority students, and new immigrant students in its public schools during that time. More 8th-graders in Connecticut were proficient in reading than in any other state. Connecticut was also the top-performing state in writing, and globally, only top-ranked Singapore outscored Connecticut's students in science. The achievement gap between White students and students of color decreased, and the more than 25% of Connecticut students who were Black or Latinx substantially outperformed their counterparts nationally.

In explaining Connecticut's strong achievement gains, the National Education Goals Panel cited the state's equity-oriented teacher policies as a critical element, pointing to the 1986 Education Enhancement Act as the linchpin of these reforms.[30] Following the recommendations of a blue-ribbon commission appointed by the governor, this omnibus bill coupled major increases in teacher salaries with higher standards for teacher education and licensing and substantial investments in mentoring for beginning teachers and professional development for all staff. An initial investment of $300 million—the result of a state surplus—was used to boost minimum beginning teacher salaries in an equalizing fashion that gave more money to low-wealth districts. Funds were allocated based on district need and the number of fully certified teachers, creating incentives for districts to recruit those who had met the new high certification standards and for individuals to meet these standards. Salary schedules remained locally bargained, and the new minimum created a floor on which the rest of the schedule was raised.

Because of these incentives, the state was able to eliminate emergency credentials. To ensure an adequate supply of qualified teachers, the state offered incentives, including scholarships and forgivable loans, to attract high-ability teacher candidates—especially for those who teach in high-demand fields and for teachers of color—and encouraged well-qualified teachers from other states to come to Connecticut by creating license reciprocity. These initiatives quickly eliminated teacher shortages, even in the cities, and created surpluses of teachers within 3 years of their enactment. This allowed districts, including those in the cities, to be highly selective in their hiring and demanding in their on-the-job expectations for teacher expertise.

While it was enhancing incentives to teach, the state raised teacher education and licensing standards by requiring a major in the discipline to be taught plus extensive knowledge of teaching and learning—including knowledge about literacy development and the teaching of special needs students. Candidates also participated in a state-funded mentoring program in their first 2 years on the job. During this time, they received support from trained mentor teachers and completed a sophisticated portfolio assessment through which state-trained assessors determined what additional mentoring might be needed and, ultimately, who could continue in teaching. The focus of teaching practice was on deeper learning for students, with an emphasis on critical thinking, problem-solving, and inquiry.

New standards for students were also enacted, accompanied by assessments that included open-ended performance tasks that called for critical thinking and communication skills. In 2000, the state launched an Early Reading Success initiative to train a cadre of literacy experts in the use of diagnostic assessments and individualized instruction for priority high-need schools. The training expanded over time to include all educators in priority schools. The state provided targeted resources to the neediest districts, including funding for professional development for teachers and administrators, preschool and all-day kindergarten for students, and smaller teacher–student ratios, among other supports.

A National Education Goals Panel report found that in high-need districts with sharply improved achievement, educators cited the high quality of teachers and administrators as a critical reason for their gains and noted that even at a time when other states across the country were experiencing shortages, "when there is a teaching opening in a Connecticut elementary school, there are often several hundred applicants."[31]

Other civil rights litigation around access to teachers has occurred in cities such as Los Angeles and New York City, spurring efforts to increase incentives to teach in high-need communities to equalize access to qualified teachers. When New York State was held accountable for more equitable funding, supporting salary increases and investments in teacher preparation and mentoring in New York City, schools serving the highest-need students saw a sharp increase in the proportion of experienced and certified teachers in their schools, which transformed student achievement outcomes.[32]

At the federal level, the Civil Rights Data Collection provides information on the percentage of inexperienced and uncertified teachers in relation to the proportion of students of color in those schools. These data are used to inform both federal investigations of equitable access and state actions. The "comparability" provisions of the Elementary and Secondary Education Act (currently known as the Every Student Succeeds Act, or ESSA) are aimed at ensuring that children from low-income families are not taught by more inexperienced, out-of-field, or ineffective teachers than those in more affluent schools within the same district. Though currently unenforced at the federal level, this provision offers another lever for attention at the state and local levels and could become a more powerful tool in a future federal administration. Currently, ESSA requires each state to develop an Equity Plan explaining how it will create more equitable access to teachers who are fully prepared and credentialed. These provisions offer an opportunity to secure stronger teaching for students, but more is needed to be sure teachers are prepared to teach equitably and to teach for deeper learning.[33]

A MARSHALL PLAN FOR TEACHING

In high-performing countries, a coherent set of policies supporting teacher recruitment, preparation, compensation, and ongoing development build an infrastructure that enables teaching in support of deeper learning and equity to become the norm.[34] Most now provide high-quality graduate-level teacher education designed to ensure that teachers can effectively educate all of their students. Preparation is usually fully subsidized for all entrants and includes a year of practice teaching in a clinical school connected to the university, much like a teaching hospital. Schools receive funding to provide coaching, seminars, classroom visits, and joint planning time for beginners as well as veterans. Salaries are competitive with other professions, offering additional stipends for hard-to-staff locations.

Effective action to ensure that all students have well-qualified teachers can be modeled after practices in medicine. Since 1944, the federal government has subsidized medical training to fill shortages and build teaching hospitals and training programs in high-need areas. A robust national teacher quality and supply policy, on the order of the post-World War II Marshall Plan, could be accomplished for less than 5% of the 2022 defense budget of $778 billion and, in a matter of only a few years, establish a stable, highly competent teaching force in all communities.

Such a plan would require, first, that the federal government expand *service scholarships and loan forgiveness* programs to fully cover preparation costs at the undergraduate and graduate levels for recruits who teach in a high-need field or location for at least 4 years. (After 3 years, teachers are more likely to remain in the profession and make a difference for student achievement.) Because fully prepared novices are twice as likely to stay in teaching as those who lack training, shortages caused by annual churn could be reduced rapidly if districts could hire better-prepared teachers. Virtually all of the vacancies currently filled with emergency teachers could be filled with well-prepared teachers if 50,000 scholarships or loans fully covering teachers' preparation were available to enable entry into teaching each year.

Second, as in medicine, the Marshall plan should support *improved preparation, including teaching schools that function like teaching hospitals.* Just as teaching hospitals that train doctors for state-of-the-art practice are supported by federal funding through Medicare and Medicaid, teaching schools attached to universities that demonstrate best practices, like those we have described, should be funded to enable candidates to learn how to teach diverse learners well. Effective models have already been created by universities sponsoring professional development schools and by school districts offering urban teacher residencies that place candidates with expert teachers in schools designed to support them while they complete their coursework.[35] These schools should be those that instantiate student-centered, deeper learning practices with the wraparound supports that enable student success, so that new practitioners can learn how to create a path to equity rather than unwittingly replicating the dysfunctional status quo because that is all they have seen and experienced.

Third, providing high-quality *mentoring for all beginning teachers* would sharply reduce attrition and increase competence. With one-third of new teachers leaving within 5 years, and rates much higher for those who are underprepared and who lack mentoring,[36] recruitment efforts are like pouring water into a leaky bucket. A federal matching grant to states and districts that create high-quality mentoring and induction programs for beginning teachers—who most often teach in high-need schools—would reduce churn, heighten teaching quality, and heighten student achievement.

Fourth, *recruitment incentives* should be designed to attract and retain expert, experienced teachers who can provide teaching and mentoring in high-need schools, such as those certified by the National Board for Professional Teaching Standards. These teachers have been found to be highly effective as teachers, mentors, and colleagues, raising the level of practice and student outcomes in their classrooms and schools.[37] Federal matching grants could leverage policies like those recently adopted in California, which offer stipends of $5,000 annually for Board-certified teachers who work in high-poverty schools, so that they can help support new teachers and other colleagues to reduce attrition and enhance the quality of teaching.

Finally, *federal tax credits for teachers* could begin to level the compensation playing field for teaching in comparison to other professions. Refundable tax credits to early education and public K–12 educators could be used to help attract, retain, and grow a well-prepared and diverse educator workforce, and to incentivize service in high-need areas where there are less state and local resources than in wealthier areas. For example, early childhood educators and educators teaching in high-need public schools could receive the maximum credit of $15,000, which would boost the average K–12 teacher's salary by 25% and the average preschool teacher's salary by nearly 50%, lifting them out of near-poverty status. Other K–12 public school educators would receive a credit based on a sliding scale determined by how many students from low-income families are served in their schools. In the long run, these programs would save far more than they cost. The savings would include the more than $7 billion dollars now wasted annually because of high teacher turnover, plus the even higher costs of grade retention, summer school, remedial programs, lost wages, and prison sentences for dropouts (another $50 billion, increasingly tied to illiteracy and school failure). A Marshall Plan for Teaching could help ensure that the U.S. can place well-qualified teachers in the schools that most need them and give all students a genuine opportunity to learn.

CHAPTER 6

High-Quality Curriculum

Deeper learning has historically been the province of the advantaged—those who could afford to send their children to the best private schools and to live in the most desirable school districts. Research on both inequality across schools and tracking within schools has suggested that students in more affluent schools and top tracks are given the kind of problem-solving education that befits the future managerial class, whereas students in lower tracks and higher-poverty schools are given the kind of rule-following tasks that mirror much of factory and other working-class work. To the degree that race mirrors class, these inequalities in access to deeper learning are shortchanging Black and Latino/a students.

—Jal Mehta, "Deeper Learning Has a Race Problem"[1]

In the article quoted above, Harvard University Professor Jal Mehta noted that "deeper learning has a race problem." The inquiry-based "thinking curriculum" that supports deeper learning has not been made available to all students and has been especially inaccessible to students of color, who are often segregated in schools that offer a lower-level curriculum and, in these and other settings, are underrepresented in gifted and talented programs and advanced courses in which deeper learning practices are more likely to be found.[2]

INEQUALITIES IN ACCESS TO DEEPER LEARNING

As with so many other inequities, there are historical roots to this problem. The famous debates between W. E. B. Du Bois and Booker T. Washington took up the issue of whether Black students should be educated to think critically and control the course of their own learning or be educated for farm and trade work. From a practical standpoint, Washington's argument that education for Black citizens could be designed to prepare them for the roles assigned to them in Southern society was aimed at encouraging White legislators and philanthropists to feel comfortable investing in Black schools. Du Bois's advocacy for a liberal education that developed thinking skills was threatening to many for the same reason that allowing enslaved people to read had been outlawed. It is more difficult to oppress an educated people.[3]

In addition to schools separated by de jure and then de facto segregation, tracking systems were developed in the early 1990s to separate students within school buildings according to decisions made about the specific vocations they would be enabled to hold. These tracks were justified by eugenicists' "evidence" about differential intelligence. Psychologist and IQ test developer Lewis Terman, a professor at Stanford University, declared that 80% of the immigrants he tested appeared to be "feeble-minded," and he concluded the following in his 1922 book *Intelligence Tests and School Reorganization*:

> Their dullness seems to be racial, or at least in the family stock from which they come. The fact one meets this type with such extraordinary frequency among Indians, Mexicans, and negroes suggests quite forcibly that the whole question of racial differences in mental differences will have to be taken up anew. . . . Children of this group should be segregated in special classes. . . . They cannot master abstractions, but they can often be made efficient workers.[4]

Schools were designed to be mechanisms for efficient sorting of manpower in the industrialized economy. As educator W. B. Pillsbury wrote in *Scientific Monthly* in 1921:

> We can picture the educational system as having a very important function as a selecting agency, a means of selecting the men of best intelligence from the deficient and mediocre. All are poured into the system at the bottom; the incapable are soon rejected or drop out after repeating various grades and pass into the ranks of unskilled labor. . . . The more intelligent who are to be clerical workers pass into the high school; the most intelligent enter the universities whence they are selected for the professions.[5]

The conception of schools as selecting only a few for thinking work rather than as developing the talents of all to a high level has remained, even as educational expectations in the society and the labor market have changed dramatically. As a result of the work of the scientific managers in the early 1900s, tracking in U.S. schools starts much earlier and is much more extensive than in most other countries, where differentiation of curriculum does not occur until high school. The result of this practice is that challenging curricula are rationed to a very small proportion of students, and far fewer U.S. students ever encounter the kinds of deeper learning opportunities students in high-achieving countries typically experience.[6]

In recent years, the test-based accountability system introduced by No Child Left Behind (NCLB) reinforced both tracking and its focus on low-level skills for those in the bottom tracks. While NCLB brought a needed measure of attention to the achievement of often-neglected groups of students, high-stakes testing using the tools that were required of states during this era inadvertently reinforced long-standing differentials in access to meaningful curriculum. This occurred for at least two reasons. First, in many schools, especially those serving students from low-income families, the curriculum was narrowed to mirror the multiple-choice tests featuring low-level questions[7] on which students needed to perform well to avoid school sanctions and, in some cases, to support salaries and continued employment for staff.[8]

Second, the tests have long been used as a way of allocating differential access to the curriculum to different groups of students, with students of color and students from low-income families generally relegated to remedial, rote-oriented courses of study based primarily on their scores. In many cases, these courses use a highly scripted curriculum that leaves little room for enriching, hands-on, higher-order learning.[9] Furthermore, schools serving predominantly students of color have been found to offer more remedial and vocational courses for low-status occupations rather than advanced or high-status technical educational options.[10] These conditions frequently undermine student motivation, efficacy, achievement, and access to opportunity and are out of step with young people's developmental needs and educational rights.[11] In addition, lower-level courses are often taught by inexperienced and underprepared teachers, who also tend to leave the profession quickly.

HOW ACCESS TO DEEPER LEARNING CAN BE SECURED

Access to a deeper learning curriculum should begin in preschool, when children are developing their initial brain architecture as they explore, inquire, communicate, and play.[12] Children are innately creative and are always engaged in problem-solving, acquiring knowledge and putting it to use. High-quality preschool curriculum and instruction cultivates these deeper learning abilities, along with social–emotional skills, so that they transfer into approaches to learning throughout later schooling and life.

Investment in quality preschool for historically underresourced children has been found to have crucial benefits, including improvements in traditional measures, such as stronger reading and math skills; a reduced need for special education; increased high school graduation, college attendance, and completion rates; and increased parental involvement and healthier lifestyles.[13] As Nobel Prize–winning economist James Heckman has noted, every dollar invested in a high-quality early childhood education produces returns of 13% annually and a benefit–cost ratio of more than 7 to 1 as a function of stronger employment and reduced social costs for participants later in life.[14] Longitudinal studies find that participation in preschool also develops key workforce skills, for which "remedies later in life—such as job training programs and second-chance GED programs—are prohibitively costly in comparison."[15]

Despite the societal returns, however, according to the U.S. Department of Education's 2013 Equity Commission, "Fewer than half (48%) of poor children are ready for school at age 5, compared with 75% of children from families with moderate and high income."[16] By contrast "The world's best-performing systems make [access to preschool] universal."[17]

Researchers have identified key characteristics of programs that work well. In early learning, teachers with specialized training in early childhood teaching get better results,[18] and "preschool students benefit from intentional teaching focused on specific learning goals and academic content, [as well as] from deep learning opportunities through discovery and social interaction."[19] In addition, small class sizes and low teacher–student ratios make a positive difference for individualizing support for students.[20] Access to quality preschool has increasingly been part of the remedy in school finance lawsuits addressing inequities.

Building on these early experiences, elementary and secondary schools that successfully support deeper learning for students of color and those from low-income communities engage in a number of common practices. These include:

- authentic instruction and assessment (e.g., project-based and collaborative learning, performance-based assessment, and connections to relevant topics related to student identities and the world beyond school);
- personalized supports for learning (e.g., advisory systems, differentiated instruction, and social and emotional learning and skill-building); and
- supports for educator learning through reflection, collaboration, leadership, and professional development.[21]

In untracked settings in which students are receiving a message that all can succeed, they engage in mastery learning experiences through which they undertake meaningful questions, conduct inquiries together, present and vet their answers to one another, and continue to revise their findings and products until they have more deeply understood the concepts. By revising their work, students learn that they can become competent by applying purposeful effort (often guided by rubrics that identify what they have done well and what is left to do), and they develop cognitive strategies that they can transfer to future work. In many of these schools, students publicly present exhibitions or portfolios of their work at the end of a grade level or for graduation to demonstrate how they are mastering competencies that guide a school's curriculum. As students take agency in the learning process, they come to understand both how they learn and what they care about, which propels their work going forward. They develop a growth mindset and the motivation to continue to define questions and pursue deeper learning about matters they care about, including pathways to college and careers.

One example that has scaled significantly is the network of Linked Learning schools—which now number more than 600 in California—that were launched as a district-supported redesign of education by the Irvine Foundation and expanded through a $500 million Career Pathways Trust enacted by the legislature to stimulate the design and implementation of these models. The models are typically new small schools or academies within a larger school building that integrate rigorous academics with career-based learning and real-world workplace experiences. They include schools with themes and industry relationships ranging from engineering and medical sciences to arts, technology, and law, among many others.

These student-centered environments eliminate the divide between academic and vocational tracks that once divided students substantially by race and class. They emphasize supportive relationships between students and teachers in academic environments that are challenging, relevant, collaborative, and student-directed. Students are assessed on their mastery of knowledge and skills through projects connected to real-life situations, and they have multiple opportunities to demonstrate that mastery. The schools are connected to their communities through industry partners and relationships with other community organizations that provide internships and other learning opportunities and participate in evaluating authentic student work. Educators are supported in creating a student-centered learning environment as they design their specific pathway and regularly evolve their work with feedback from student surveys and other insights. This is the type of setting necessary for students to develop the skills to succeed in college, career, and life. Below we describe how two of these schools are organized and how they succeed.

LINKED LEARNING IN ACTION

Dozier-Libbey Medical High School, a small district-run school in the Antioch School District (between San Francisco and Stockton in Northern California), is located on the edge of town amid cow pastures and near several medical centers. The student population is 78% students of color, and most come from low-income families. The district created the small school in 2008 in response to district overcrowding and following an assessment of the highest community employment opportunities.

As part of California's Linked Learning initiative, which eliminates the divide between college and career preparation, the school offers a rigorous college preparatory curriculum in which students engage in hands-on, applied, and interdisciplinary experiences consistently infused with a health care focus. All students are enabled to take the coursework necessary to make them eligible for the University of California system, including a minimum of four math courses and four science courses. Teachers' steadfast commitment to mastery rather than rigid adherence to a pacing guide, coupled with in-class supports for struggling students, enables all students to access and deeply understand the curriculum. The vast majority of DLMHS students graduate (97%), and 96% complete the college prep program. About 90% go on to college immediately; others work in skilled jobs to support themselves and their families until they can afford higher education. The students' test scores and growth rates on tests substantially exceed those for similar students in their district and the state.

This is possible because students are well-supported to undertake work that is intellectually challenging and meaningful. For example, 12th-grade students examine medical ethics across academic disciplines, reading *The Immortal Life of Henrietta Lacks* in English class; learning about eugenics and medical experimentation in Medical Ethics class; and developing, designing, and building a device to address a disability in Physics. Students write a paper on who benefits, who is harmed, and the cost of making their medical device. In a culminating project, they investigate the meaning of disability and the biases in the notions of "fixing" a disability.

As the principal notes, "The curriculum is important, but the process is the most important thing because we don't even know what they're going to need to know or learn. They need to learn the learning process. So that's why we really heavily emphasize project-based learning, cooperative learning, presentations. We try to have [students] interact with adults as much as possible so they can sharpen those communication skills. We give them a lot of opportunity for public speaking so that they have those kinds of skills that they're going to need for whatever field they go into that we don't even know, might not exist yet."

Students have multiple opportunities to demonstrate their learning in ways that correspond to their strengths. And teachers design the work so that they can provide supports. For example, a 12th-grade English teacher finds that the process of having her students write their college personal statements at the beginning of the year reveals much to her about her students' lives. She draws on what she learns to provide accommodations for her students. For example, one year she had a student with Tourette's syndrome and a very hard life. She said:

> He basically went into foster care because he was a drug mule between his parents and his parents' clients and he was sleeping in a car for a year and a half. I mean just unbelievable. So we developed a little [system] where he would look at me and he'd [give a hand gesture when] he needed time outside to just make whatever go away.

She went on to explain that although she starts the year by setting high behavioral standards, after she reads the essays, she realizes that making individual accommodations can be beneficial to particular students. Providing students with that level of respect means that they do not take advantage of the situation. "They're not asking for the moon, and they never would," she says. This particular student's life trajectory was likely transformed by the care he received from his teachers.

He shared: "I developed Tourette's in 10th grade. I blank a lot, can't focus on the lesson. Teachers have really helped me out. I let them in, and they helped me out. I was gone 3 weeks a bunch of times so I got really behind. I never thought I would catch up, but my teachers helped me out and now I am going to graduate."

Believing in the potential of every student has enabled the principal and staff to create a culture of caring and respect between and among teachers and students. The combination of purpose, engagement, and compassion creates a deeper learning setting that also supports equity.

Life Academy is another certified Linked Learning pathway, enacted by a small public high school in Oakland Unified School District, that weaves student-centeredness into nearly every aspect of its work and culture. Its goal is to prepare its students to become future health professionals within the biological sciences. The school's focus on students is evidenced through college and career preparation coursework, inquiry-based pedagogy, health/science career internships, a 4-year advisory program, multiple performance-based exhibitions that include an interdisciplinary and scholarly senior exhibition, and a wide array of student-interest-driven "post-session" classes at the end of the year.

Life Academy was the first new high school opened during Oakland's community-driven movement for small autonomous schools in the 2000s. Opening in the fall of 2001, the health academy was designed based on research about effective small learning communities, and it was originally housed within a large comprehensive high school. The directors worked with families and community members as well as biotech and health care companies to design a school that would be safe, hold students to high standards, and prepare them to work in the health care and bioscience fields.

Life Academy's stated mission is "to dramatically interrupt patterns of injustice and inequity for underserved communities in Oakland. Through transformative learning experiences focused on health, medicine, and bioscience, students are engaged in learning and inspired to acquire the skills, knowledge, and habits necessary to succeed in college and careers in the medical field." Life Academy has no separate application requirements. Instead, like nearly every high school in the Oakland Unified School District (OUSD), its students enroll through the district's citywide "options enrollment" process. After the opportunity to visit high schools with their families during the winter quarter, 9th-graders submit an options application to rank their school preferences. Life Academy's students come primarily from the surrounding neighborhood, but some come from far corners of the district.

The school does not "cream" students: The percentage of English language learners (30%) is the same as OUSD's; 99% of the school's families qualify for free or reduced-price lunch; and approximately 50% of students' parents did not complete high school. Despite these hurdles, Life Academy is realizing its mission of interrupting patterns of inequity for its students. To

79

become more effective in preparing students, the school expanded to the middle grades, serving students in grades 6-12 by 2015.

All students select one of the school's three career pathways—medicine, health, or biotechnology—and take courses and complete an internship aligned with that pathway. To support these internships, the school has developed deep relationships with several industry partners, including Oakland Children's Hospital, Youth Bridge (Alta Bates and Summit hospitals), and Highland Hospital. Besides the internships, hallmark instructional elements of the school include an emphasis on personalization, cross-disciplinary projects, public demonstration of mastery, a college preparatory curriculum, and productive group work.

The culminating work for students is the senior research paper, a year-long and multistage assignment. Each student researches a question that emerges out of an internship experience. To answer the question, each student conducts a scaled-down literature review, interviews an expert, writes a paper, and presents and defends findings to a panel that includes the advisor, students, and family or community members.

The school had a 100% graduation rate in 2020-2021, and has had the highest UC and CSU acceptance rate of any high school in Oakland, with students going to schools like Berkeley and UCLA, as well as Stanford, University of San Francisco, and Smith College.

When asked what high school experiences have contributed to their college readiness, more than 90% of Life Academy students list relationships with teachers and advisors (93%) and workplace internships (93%). They also identify aspects of the way they are encouraged to work on their projects and demonstrate mastery, including "explaining my thinking" (93%), "testing or trying out my ideas to see if they worked" (93%), "evaluating myself on my class work" (95%), "participating in peer review of work" (90%), and "having to revise my work until it meets standards of proficiency" (93%).

These practices are part of a performance-based, mastery-oriented, relationship-supported approach to learning that can create success for all students. Life Academy's focus on students drives every decision: what and how to teach authentically, what structures will equip students and teachers to know and believe in each other, and how to bring out the best of the students and their community.

Sources: Darling-Hammond, L., Friedlaender, D., & Snyder, J. (2014a). Student-centered schools: Policy supports for closing the opportunity gap. *Stanford Center for Opportunity Policy in Education.* Friedlaender, D. (2014). *Student-centered learning: Dozier-Libbey Medical High School.* Stanford Center for Opportunity Policy in Education. Richardson, N., & Feldman, J. (2014). *Student-centered learning: Life Academy of Health and Bioscience.* Stanford Center for Opportunity Policy in Education. SCOPE (2014). *Student-centered learning: How our schools are closing the opportunity gap.* Stanford Center for Opportunity Policy in Education. Case studies can be found at https://edpolicy.stanford.edu/library/publications/1175/.

The American Institutes of Research found that across a set of 13 deeper learning–focused schools in California and New York, compared with matched comparison schools, students experiencing this kind of deeper learning achieved higher scores on the international PISA (Program for International Student Assessment) test, were more likely to graduate high school in 4 years, were more likely to enroll in 4-year colleges, and were more likely to attend more selective colleges. Importantly, the accomplishments were achieved regardless of whether participating students entered high school with low or high levels of prior achievement.[22] Many other studies have confirmed these kinds of outcomes, including for students of color, students from low-income families, and students with disabilities who may begin school with less well-developed foundations but who learn deeply with a thoughtful curriculum, strong instruction, and readily available supports.[23]

When students can engage in culturally relevant learning that allows them to critically examine their experiences and cultural histories, additional benefits accrue. Studies in California have found significant academic gains for White, Black, Latinx, and Asian students taking ethnic studies courses, including large gains in attendance, grades, credits earned, graduation rates, and college enrollment.[24] A study of participation in Mexican American studies courses in Arizona found similarly positive outcomes for achievement and graduation.[25]

To the degree that deeper learning remains inaccessible and unavailable to students of color and to systemically underresourced children generally, America will never be able to solve its equity dilemma. The evidence is clear: The skills required to be truly college- and career-ready will only be obtained if students have access to a curriculum that provides ample opportunity to develop higher-order skills. The notion that students from low-income backgrounds are incapable of deeper learning has been difficult to challenge because educators in struggling schools often face a variety of obstacles related to the social context, which schools cannot address on their own. Additionally, many educators have not had access to clear and compelling examples that show how it can be done or the training to do it themselves.

Those examples now exist and can be planted in a growing number of contexts, now that networks of such successful schools are available to support public school districts in making these changes.[26] Still, there are hurdles embedded in the system we have inherited that require civil rights engagement to open the path to deeper learning.

THE CIVIL RIGHTS CONTRIBUTION AND ROAD AHEAD

The Civil Rights Data Collection provides information about access to advanced programs and coursework for schools with different proportions of students of color. These data illustrate where there is differential access to certain kinds of deeper learning opportunities and can flag for advocates, as well as districts, the kinds of inequities that need to be addressed. The data show large differences at the state and national levels in access to advanced coursework expected for college, especially in mathematics and science; these differences provide grounds for litigation and legislative action.[27]

Differential access to high-quality curriculum for students of color has been an issue raised in both school finance and desegregation litigation. One increasingly common response has been to require the provision of high-quality preschool to students from low-income families as a remedy in school finance settlements. The structures of tracking, which create segregated experiences within schools—with some students having access to a deeper learning curriculum and others getting a rote learning experience—have also been raised in the context of desegregation lawsuits[28] and of magnet school strategies that create segregated programs within schools that reserve the deeper learning benefits of magnets only to the privileged within a presumably desegregated school.[29]

Beyond these formal measures of "deeper," or at least "advanced," learning, some states, ranging from Connecticut to California, have used the opportunity ESSA provided to evaluate schools on multiple measures to report on whether, how, and to whom districts are offering a "rich" curriculum and high-quality college- and career-ready curriculum pathways. By including information regarding student access to and completion of college- and career-ready curricula in their accountability plans, states can incentivize increasing students' curriculum opportunities and reveal whether additional resources and supports are needed.[30] There is still a long road to travel to access deeper learning for many students, and the destination will depend in substantial part on high-quality education being acknowledged as a right for all.[31]

A wide-ranging set of policies is needed to create student-centered schools focused on deeper learning for diverse students. They include the standards and supports we have identified in earlier chapters of this book: expectations and enablements for healthy environments in communities and adequate resources for families; equitable school funding that prioritizes student needs; investments in social–emotional learning and restorative practices that enable safe and inclusive learning environments; and investments in educator learning, coupled with legal expectations that well-prepared educators will be available in all schools.

Additional supports for redesigning schools to accommodate these new practices are important. For example, Linked Learning schools and districts are supported by a technical assistance provider, the Linked Learning Alliance, which supports the school redesign process, offers a certification process that recognizes best practice and helps schools make progress through the concrete steps they take, offers a network that shares practices across schools and provides educators with examples and supports they need to improve continuously. School-to-school networks are a feature of federally and state-funded professional learning support that has proven successful in England, Canada, and Australia by providing schools opportunities to learn together, as well as enabling struggling schools to learn from schools that offer positive exemplars of practice.[32]

The curriculum of deeper learning schools is shaped by rigorous performance assessments that engage students in extended projects and research—often presented, exhibited, and defended publicly—that are evaluated by common rubrics and provide the occasion for students to develop and revise their work to meet schoolwide standards. Each of the schools described in this chapter has clearly articulated competencies that students need to demonstrate before graduation, along with rubrics for assessing those skills. These kinds of projects and skills—which are the basis for the students' college and career success—are evaluated in national and state assessment systems in England, Ireland, Australia, New Zealand, Singapore, and the International Baccalaureate program, and were used in U.S. assessment systems during the 1990s, until No Child Left Behind (NCLB) arrived in 2002.[33]

In the NCLB era with its greatly expanded state testing requirements and scores tied to school sanctions, many schools like these have found that the rich and relevant curriculum they seek to offer has been at odds with the expectations for multiple-choice thinking and teaching imposed by high-stakes standardized tests. As a consequence, they have had to maintain the equivalent of two curricula, teaching students to pick one answer out of five on tests of recall and recognition, while also trying to teach them to demonstrate analytical thinking and problem-solving in much more applied and authentic ways. As the RAND Corporation found when it examined these tests, 98% of the items on state math tests measured lower-level skills, as did 80% of the items on state English language arts tests.[34] Many schools—especially those serving the highest-need students whose schools stood to receive stiff sanctions, including closure, for not making "adequate yearly progress" on schools—abandoned deeper learning efforts and began to teach directly to the tests. This (ironically) lowered the quality of curriculum for students further and drove good teachers out of these schools, leaving students further behind in the effort to be ready for the complex 21st-century world that awaits them.[35]

Federal amendments to the law (now the Every Student Succeeds Act, or ESSA) to allow more instructionally useful, performance-based approaches to assessment, like those used in formal systems in other countries, are needed to support deeper learning across the country, as are investments that make it possible to offer and score those assessments comparably for purposes of equity analyses.[36] This is especially true in the schools serving the highest-need students, where stronger teaching and learning opportunities are most desperately needed.

CHAPTER 7

Conclusion

Injustice anywhere is a threat to justice everywhere. We are caught in
an inescapable network of mutuality, tied in a single garment of destiny.
Whatever affects one directly, affects all indirectly.

—Dr. Martin Luther King, Jr., "Letter From Birmingham Jail"

In the interdependent world we currently inhabit, threatened by conflict and
climate change and driven by rapidly changing knowledge and technologies,
a highly educated, communally committed populace is necessary for the survival and success of societies as well as individuals. This interdependence means
that the quest for access to an equitable, empowering education for all people
has become a critical issue for the nation as a whole. No society can thrive in
a technological, knowledge-based economy by starving large segments of its
population of learning. The path to our mutual well-being is built on equitable
educational opportunity.

As we imagine what it means to prepare the nation's future adults—people
on whom both an aging and youthful populace will rely—it is critical that we
invest in the deeper learning that enables creativity, critical thinking, collaboration, a commitment to social good, and a high capacity for ongoing learning.
The evidence shows that this is possible, but only if we can surmount the inequities that are built into every facet of our society, including its schools.

Access to deeper learning is influenced by factors both inside and outside of
schools: the contexts created by states, cities, neighborhoods, and income levels; social attitudes, beliefs, and norms; district and school investments; curriculum opportunities; access to professional training and development; and more.

At the federal and state levels, advancing the right to deeper learning requires building an interagency capacity to coordinate, execute, and monitor
whole-child policies that are focused on resource allocation and civil rights
enforcement across offices, from labor, to health and human services, to agriculture and education. More effective administrative structures that increase
efficiencies by streamlining investments and reducing redundancies can leverage opportunities to take advantage of this transformative moment. At the
school level, community school designs that integrate services on behalf of
children and families can make these investments come alive in ways that
transform lives.

The success of such an effort rests upon our ability to restore and protect our tattered social safety net for children and families, eliminating child poverty. It requires that we litigate and legislate our way to toxin-free communities that are designed for thriving whole humans with ample green space, resources, investments, and opportunities.

It also requires that we take advantage of the current moment created by the disruption of the COVID-19 pandemic to *reinvent* our system of education. We have made major scientific advancements in our understanding of human development and learning; as a nation, we are coming to see that our societal health requires us to provide *all* of our students with the sort of "thinking curriculum" we long reserved for a small elite. We are poised to claim high-quality education as a right for all.

To take advantage of this moment, we need to undo many of the policies that prop up the existing factory models designed to select and sort, rather than to develop all children's talents, and replace them with policies that encourage and allow us to enact the kinds of curricular designs, learning communities, high-quality assessments, community partnerships, and teaching practices that students deserve. There are three major areas of work ahead.

First, the civil rights road to deeper learning opportunity will require a number of efforts to end the legacy of under resourced and segregated schools. To do this, federal, state, and local governments must take these steps:

- *Provide **adequate and equitable funding** based on pupil needs*, not property tax wealth, to every district and school to support a stable, diverse, well-prepared staff, provide programmatic and curriculum resources, and ensure that all children have what they need to learn effectively.
- *Ensure that all children have access to **high-quality preschool*** that offers a deeper learning curriculum from an early age, when children are developing their initial brain architecture as they explore, inquire, communicate, and play. Children are innately curious and engaged in problem-solving, through which they acquire knowledge and put it to use. High-quality preschools cultivate these learning abilities, along with social–emotional skills, so that they transfer into learning throughout later schooling and life. Investment in quality preschool equalizes opportunity by enabling long-term academic achievement and attainment, as well as life success.
- *Foster **integration** and intergroup understanding* with strategies that enable greater diversity (such as integrative district boundaries and magnet school incentives); with curriculum that supports cultural inclusion, cross-cultural understanding, and positive relations among groups; and with actions promoting identity development and a sense of belonging for all students.
- *Support **civil rights*** by reinstating guidance for achieving school diversity and equitable treatment for students from the Departments of

Education and Justice and supporting their enforcement authority and capacity to offer technical assistance to ensure compliance with civil rights laws.

Second, within a productive policy environment, schools can do more to provide the right kinds of supports for students if they are also designed to foster strong relationships and provide a holistic approach to student supports and family engagement. Continued, stable, and expanded investments in federal and state programs promoting social–emotional learning, restorative practices, physical and mental health supports, and full-service community schools, including federal partnerships with states to create systemic initiatives, can make these essential measures the norm—viewed as part of a right to supportive education, instead of the exception. To provide settings for healthy development, educators and policymakers can take these steps:

- Design *relationship-centered schools* in which students can be well-known and supported, by creating small schools or learning communities within schools, looping teachers with students for more than one year, creating advisory systems, supporting teaching teams, and organizing schools with longer grade spans—all of which have been found to strengthen relationships and improve student attendance, achievement, and attainment. Funding allocations as well as incentive grants and professional development for school redesign can support these changes.
- Develop *curriculum, assessment, and instruction for deeper learning* that builds on prior knowledge and experience; integrates students' cultural and linguistic funds of knowledge; supports collaboration and inquiry interwoven with direct instruction; provides opportunities for authentic, formative assessment that informs reflection and revision of work; and fosters metacognitive and strategic learning that supports student agency, independence, resourcefulness, and resilience.
- Provide *expanded and enriched learning* time to ensure that students receive holistic developmental support and do not fall behind, including skillful tutoring that can replace tracking with targeted academic support and additional support for homework, mentoring, and extracurricular enrichment.
- Replace zero-tolerance policies with *positive, community-centered discipline policies* and professional development focused on explicit teaching of social–emotional strategies and restorative practices that support young people in learning key skills and developing responsibility for themselves and their community. Develop district- and schoolwide norms and supports for *safe, culturally responsive communities* that provide all students with physical and psychological safety, affirmation, and belonging, as well as opportunities to learn

social, emotional, and cognitive skills. These practices reduce bullying, conflict, and the use of exclusionary discipline; and help close disciplinary gaps while supporting student belonging, engagement, mental health, achievement, and attainment.

- *Create community schools* that organize whole-child supports promoting students' physical and mental health, social welfare, and academic success and ensure regular and authentic family engagement. All adults should focus their work around a shared conception of whole-child development within a multitiered system of support, beginning with universal designs for learning and social–emotional supports in every classroom and extending through more intensive, personalized academic and nonacademic assistance students need when they need it, without labeling or delays.
- *Prioritize and fund the engagement of families* as part of the core approach to education, including home visits and flexibly scheduled student–teacher–parent conferences in which teachers learn from parents about their children; outreach to involve families in school activities; and regular communication through positive phone calls, emails, and text messages that offer information and opportunities for partnership.

These initiatives can be reinforced by

- Federal support for states to redesign their *systems of accountability and continuous improvement* to incorporate indicators of safe and inclusive climates, student opportunities to learn, and multiple measures of learning and attainment, as signaled in recent Department of Education guidance. Such systems should emphasize indicators of students' access to educational resources: well-qualified educators, a rich curriculum, high-quality teaching, instructional materials (including digital access at home and school), a positive school climate, social–emotional and academic supports, and expert instruction for English learners, students with disabilities, and other students with particular needs. They should also include indicators of learning and progress that measure learning in authentic ways, completion of well-designed pathways to college and careers, and accomplishments such as biliteracy and civic engagement.
- Federal amendments to the law (now ESSA) to allow more instructionally useful, *performance-based approaches to assessment*, like those used in other countries. These changes are needed to support deeper learning across the country, as are investments that make it possible to offer and score those assessments comparably for purposes of equity analyses.
- Continued vigilance from the Office of Civil Rights to address disciplinary disparities that come to light through the Civil Rights Data

Collection and complaints, and the reissuance of guidance for ending exclusionary discipline and infusing restorative practices in their stead.

Finally, educators need opportunities to learn how to redesign schools and develop practices that support a positive school climate; healthy, whole-child development; and deeper learning experiences. To accomplish this, policymakers and educators can take these steps:

- *Redesign **licensing and accreditation** requirements* for teachers and administrators to incorporate educator competencies regarding how to teach for deeper learning and for equity, incorporating culturally responsive and culturally competent practices; support for students' social, emotional, and cognitive development; and restorative practices.
- *Design and resource preservice **preparation programs*** for both teachers and administrators that provide a strong foundation in child and adolescent development and learning; knowledge of how to create engaging, effective instruction; skills for implementing social–emotional learning and restorative justice programs; and an understanding of how to work with families and community organizations to create a shared developmentally supportive approach. These should include year-long well-supervised clinical experiences in equity-oriented partner schools that are good models of developmentally supportive practices and that create a positive school climate for all students. Administrator preparation programs should help leaders learn how to design and foster such environments.
- *Offer widely available **professional learning opportunities*** that help educators continually build on and refine student-centered teaching and learning practices focused on deeper learning; learn to use data about school climate and a wide range of student outcomes to undertake continuous improvement; problem-solve around the needs of individual children; engage in schoolwide initiatives in collegial teams and professional learning communities; learn from other schools through networks, site visits, and documentation of successes; and develop the high levels of emotional management, communication skill, and sophistication in practice required to be responsive to all children's developmental learning needs. This requires changes to staffing and scheduling designs so that teachers have dedicated time for collaborative planning, learning, and continuous reflection.
- *Invest in educator **recruitment and retention**,* including forgivable loans and service scholarships that support strong preparation, high-retention pathways into the profession—such as residencies—that diversify the educator workforce, high-quality mentoring for beginners, and collegial environments for practice. Educator wellness investments are also key, including reasonable workloads, access to tools like mindfulness, and social–emotional learning approaches that benefit

both adults and children. A strong, stable, diverse, well-prepared teaching and leadership workforce is perhaps the most important ingredient for a positive school climate that supports effective whole-child education.

A wide-ranging set of policies is needed to create student-centered schools focused on deeper learning for all students. They include expectations and enablements for healthy environments in communities and equitable resources for families; equitable school funding that prioritizes student needs; investments in social–emotional learning and restorative practices that enable safe and inclusive learning environments; and investments in educator learning, coupled with legal expectations that well-prepared educators will be available in all schools.

Time and again, educators have demonstrated that access to supportive learning conditions and opportunities, well-resourced schools, inclusivity and affirmation, skillful teaching, and innovative, high-quality curriculum unlocks and enlivens students' potential to bloom.

The path to this vision includes civil rights enforcement related to our environment, neighborhoods, schools, and districts. It requires innovation and reimagining—dreaming beyond what we have already seen. It begins with access to safety, a stable and healthy environment, educational opportunity, and a vast future full of possibility. It continues with intellectual, social, and emotional support that enables children to take advantage of those affordances. It is sustained by a commitment to the well-being and futures of all of our children and to the ongoing work needed to remove barriers and advance the possibilities for equitable and empowering education for all.

The challenge ahead is to assemble the whole village—families, policy makers, educators, health care providers, youth developers, and philanthropists—to work together to create developmentally-grounded, equity-focused policies and practices that ensure every young person receives the benefit of what is known about how to support their healthy path to a vibrant future.

Notes

Chapter 1

1. P. L. Carter & Welner (2013), p. 1.
2. Carnevale & Rose (2015), p. 24.
3. Carnevale et al. (2013); U.S. Bureau of Labor Statistics (2022).
4. Hewlett Foundation (2013).
5. Hewlett Foundation (2013).
6. Baldwin (2020).
7. L. Darling-Hammond (2010).
8. L. Darling-Hammond et al. (2014b).
9. Tyack (1974), p. xx.
10. For a thorough treatment of this important educational history, see Adams (2020). See also Prucha (2014).
11. See Valencia (2005).
12. Johnson (2019). See also L. Darling-Hammond (2001); Johnson (2011); Schwartz (2010).
13. Hallinan (1998); Linn & Welner (2007); Mickelson (2008); Mickelson & Nkomo (2012); Wells et al. (2016).
14. Balfanz & Legters (2004); Schofield (2001); Swanson (2004).
15. Johnson (2019).
16. Bridges (2018).
17. See Bristol & Martin-Fernandez (2019).
18. Durlak et al. (2011); Payton et al. (2008); Taylor et al. (2017).
19. Hurtado (2005); Kurlaender & Yun (2007); Mickelson & Nkomo (2012); Page (2008).
20. Braddock & Gonzalez (2010); Braddock & McPartland (1989).
21. Center for American Progress (2011).
22. *Opening Doors, Expanding Opportunities* (2016); see also George & Darling-Hammond (2019).
23. Brittain, Willis, & Cookson (2019).

Chapter 2

1. Milman (2018).
2. Marshall & Ruane (2021).
3. Santos et al. (2021).
4. Shapiro, T. M. (2017); see also, for example, Rothstein (2004).

5. P. L. Carter & Welner (2013).
6. Rothstein (2017).
7. U.S. Census Bureau (2012).
8. U.S. Department of Education (2013), p. 30
9. Chen & Thomson (2021)
10. Pastor & Morello-Frosch (2018), p. 2.
11. Pastor & Morello-Frosch (2018), p. 2; Pulido (2000); Ringquist (2005).
12. Pastor et al. (2004), p. 280.
13. Pastor et al. (2004), p. 282.
14. Pastor et al. (2004), p. 284.
15. Pastor et al. (2004), p. 273.
16. Seligman et al. (1997); Smith (1999); Subramanian et al. (2002).
17. Adisa-Farrar (2021).
18. Adisa-Farrar (2021).
19. For a detailed analysis of how the water source decision-making unfolded, see Guyette (2017).
20. Ruckart et al. (2019), p. 3.
21. American Civil Liberties Union–Michigan (2015).
22. Ruckart et al. (2019).
23. Davis et al. (2016).
24. Ruckart et al. (2019), p. 2.
25. Hanna-Atisha et al. (2016).
26. Hanna-Atisha et al. (2016).
27. Educational Services for Children Affected by Lead Expert Panel (2015).
28. Green (2019).
29. Green (2019).
30. American Civil Liberties Union–Michigan. (2020); *D.R. v. Michigan Department of Education* (2017); Green (2019); Mitchell (2019).
31. Green (2019).
32. Cohen Milstein Sellers & Toll PLLC (2021).
33. Guyette (2018).
34. L. Darling-Hammond (2007).
35. Fortner (2021); Nelson (2016).
36. Fortner (2021).
37. Nelson (2016).
38. Nelson (2016).
39. Craddock et al. (2019).
40. Mitchell (2019).
41. Fortner (2021).
42. Garza (2021).
43. Locke et al. (2021), p. 1.
44. Hoffman et al. (2020), pp. 1–2, 11.
45. Lakhani (2020).
46. Lakhani (2020).
47. Franke (2014).
48. L. Darling-Hammond et al. (2019).
49. Milam et al. (2010); see also Krivo et al. (2009).

50. K. Darling-Hammond et al. (2020).
51. L. Darling-Hammond & Cook-Harvey (2018).
52. Centers for Disease Control and Prevention (2021).
53. K. Darling-Hammond (2021).
54. See also *Bean v. Southwestern Waste Management Corp.* (1979); Bullard (1996). More than a dozen lawsuits have been filed on behalf of residents of Flint, MI.
55. Michigan in the World and the Environmental Justice HistoryLab (2017).
56. Bullard (1983).
57. Bullard (2004).
58. Lombardi et al. (2015).
59. Weiss (2017).
60. Infrastructure Investment and Jobs Act of 2021.
61. Rubinkam (2021).
62. Tankersley et al. (2020).
63. Bailey & Duquettte (2014).
64. Volsky (2014).
65. L. Darling-Hammond (2018), p. 1.
66. Fox et al. (2014).
67. Szmigiera (2021).
68. Office of the Assistant Secretary for Planning and Evaluation (2022).
69. Cookson & Darling-Hammond (2022).
70. Ekono et al. (2016).
71. Cookson & Darling-Hammond (2022); Shaefer et al. (n.d.).
72. Children's Defense Fund (2021).
73. Parolin et al. (2021).
74. Center on Poverty & Social Policy, Columbia University (2022).

Chapter 3

1. U.S. Department of Education (2013).
2. This section draws on L. Darling-Hammond (2010).
3. *Brown v. Board of Education* (1954).
4. Cremin (1970), pp. 411–412.
5. Tyack (1974), p. 110.
6. For a summary of cases that paved the way to the *Brown* decision, see United States Courts (n.d.).
7. L. Darling-Hammond (2018).
8. Bridges (2018), p. 442.
9. Bridges (2018), pp. 444–447.
10. Orfield et al. (2016).
11. Farrie & Sciarra (2021).
12. Mathewson (2020).
13. L. Darling-Hammond (2018), p. 1.
14. Anyon (1997), p. 136; Centolanza (1986), p. 524.
15. Quoted in Anyon (1997), p. 137.
16. Anyon (1997), p. 136.
17. Barton et al. (1991), p. 9.
18. *Abbott v. Burke* (1990), 376.

19. *Abbott v. Burke* (1990), 364.
20. Anyon (1997), pp. 144–145.
21. *Williams v. State of California*, 58–66.
22. Hanushek (2003), p. 4.
23. Wise (1965).
24. *San Antonio Independent School District v. Rodriguez* (1973).
25. L. Darling-Hammond (2010), Ch. 5; L. Darling-Hammond (2019); U.S. Department of Education (2013)
26. McUsic, 1991, p. 307.
27. Farrie & Sciarra (2021).
28. Downes et al. (2009), p. 5; Guryan (2001); Nguyen-Hoang & Yinger (2014), p. 297.
29. L. Darling-Hammond (2019), p. 13.
30. L. Darling-Hammond (2019), p. 13.
31. Jackson et al. (2014).
32. Johnson (2011).
33. Mickelson & Bottia (2010).
34. Mickelson (2016).
35. George & Darling-Hammond (2019), pp. 6–7.
36. Orfield et al. (2016).
37. Frankenberg et al. (2017).
38. *Grutter v. Bollinger* (2003), quoted in *Parents Involved in Cmty. Schs. v. Seattle Sch. Dist. No. 1* (2007). 551 U.S. 701, 723 (2007), quoting Grutter v. Bollinger, 539 U.S. 306, 330 (2003).
39. Felton (2017).
40. Brittain et al. (2019).
41. Bridges (2018), p. 446.

Chapter 4

1. Quoted in S. Darling-Hammond (forthcoming).
2. Cantor et al. (2019).
3. Adapted from L. Darling-Hammond & Cook-Harvey (2018), p. 19.
4. National Scientific Council on the Developing Child (2010); Vogel & Schwabe (2016).
5. Jennings & Greenberg (2009), p. 515.
6. Melnick et al. (2017).
7. National School Climate Center (n.d.).
8. Berkowitz et al. (2016).
9. Dweck & Yeager (2019).
10. Durlak et al. (2011), pp. 3–4.
11. Advancement Project et al. (2005); Kosciw et al. (2017); Wald & Losen (2003).
12. L. Darling-Hammond, Cook-Harvey, et al. (2018), pp. 18–19; see also National Scientific Council on the Developing Child (2010).
13. Astor et al. (2009).
14. MacFarlane & Woolfson (2013).
15. MacFarlane & Woolfson (2013), p. 52.
16. Steinberg et al. (2015).

17. L. Darling-Hammond & Cook-Harvey (2018), p. 13.
18. Comer et al. (1996).
19. L. Darling-Hammond, Cook-Harvey, et al. (2018), p. 9.
20. L. Darling-Hammond, Cook-Harvey, et al. (2018), pp. 44–45.
21. Collaborative for Academic, Social, and Emotional Learning (n.d.); see also Osher et al. (2010).
22. Durlak et al. (2011); Taylor et al. (2017).
23. Tate (2019).
24. Tate (2019).
25. Adapted from Comer and Savo (2009), reported in L. Darling-Hammond et al. (2018), p. 72.
26. L. Darling-Hammond & Oakes (2019).
27. Steinberg et al. (2015).
28. Konold et al. (2017); Voight et al. (2015).
29. For a robust reading list about discrimination, exclusionary discipline, and the school-to-prison pipeline, see P. Carter et al. (2016).
30. Amemiya et al. (2020); Raffaele Mendez & Knoff (2003); Theriot & Dupper (2010).
31. Leung et al. (2022).
32. Fenning & Rose (2007); Kelly (2010); Skiba et al. (2002); Skiba & Sprague (2008); U.S. Commission on Civil Rights (2013); U.S. Commission on Civil Rights (2019).
33. U.S. Commission on Civil Rights (2019).
34. U.S. Department of Education Office for Civil Rights (2021).
35. Gilliam et al. (2016).
36. Gilliam (2016).
37. U.S. Department of Education Office for Civil Rights (2021).
38. U. S. Commission on Civil Rights (2019), p. 118.
39. Lassen et al. (2006).
40. Fabelo et al. (2011); Losen & Gillespie (2012).
41. Advancement Project et al. (2005); U.S. Commission on Civil Rights (2019), pp. 4–5, 9–10; Wald & Losen (2003).
42. Advancement Project et al. (2005); Fabelo et al. (2011); Losen & Gillespie (2012); U.S. Commission on Civil Rights (2019); Wald & Losen (2003).
43. Advancement Project et al. (2005); Fabelo et al. (2011); Kim et al. (2010); Losen & Gillespie (2012), p. 6; Losen et al. (2014); Redfield & Nance (2016); Thurlow et al. (2002); U.S. Commission on Civil Rights (2019), p. 6; Wald & Losen (2003).
44. Fabelo et al. (2011); Losen & Gillespie (2012), p. 42.
45. U.S. Department of Education Office for Civil Rights (2021).
46. Anderson et al. (2017); Loveless (2017); Morris & Perry (2016); Rausch et al. (2005); Whisman & Hammer (2014).
47. American Psychological Association Zero Tolerance Task Force (2008); Losen & Gillespie (2012).
48. Contractor & Staats (2014); Losen & Gillespie (2012).
49. American Psychological Association Zero Tolerance Task Force (2008).
50. Harry & Klingner (2006); Kim et al. (2010); Losen & Gillespie (2012); Osher et al. (2010).

51. Schott Foundation et al. (2014).
52. Klevan (2021).
53. Advocates for Children and Youth (2006); Boccanfuso & Kuhfeld (2011) (this re-
    search brief summarizes a variety of empirical research and literature on reducing
    punitive measures in discipline policies); Horner et al. (2009); Losen & Gillespie
    (2012); Sugai & Horner (2002); U.S. Commission on Civil Rights (2019).
54. Augustine et al. (2018); Fronius et al. (2019); Klevan (2021).
55. Durlak et al. (2011).
56. Losen & Gillespie (2012). "An ecological classroom-management approach deals
    with school discipline by increasing the strength and quality of classroom activi-
    ties. Some of its defining characteristics are well-planned lessons, varied methods
    of instruction, clear and developmentally appropriate behavioral expectations,
    and the careful monitoring of student engagement, with effective empathetic re-
    sponses designed to re-engage students and avoid escalation of conflicts" (Losen &
    Gillespie,2012, p. 44).
57. Christle et al. (2005); Fishman & Hack (2012); Office of Special Education Pro-
    grams Technical Assistance Center (2015); Schiff & Bazemore (2012); Simonsen
    et al. (2015).
58. L. Darling-Hammond, Cook-Harvey, et al. (2018); Learning Policy Institute &
    Turnaround for Children (2021).
59. U.S. Department of Education (2013), p. 32; see also Basch (2011).
60. Maier et al. (2017).
61. U.S. Department of Education Office for Civil Rights (2016). Particular suspen-
    sion rates by race and gender include Native American/Alaska Native (23%),
    Native Hawaiian/Pacific Islander (23%), Black (25%), multiracial boys with dis-
    abilities (27%), and multiracial girls with disabilities (21%).
62. U.S. Commission on Civil Rights (2019).
63. U.S. Department of Education (2015), p. 131.
64. U.S. Department of Justice, Civil Rights Division, & U.S. Department of Educa-
    tion Office for Civil Rights (2014), pp. 5–6.
65. Redfield & Nance (2016).
66. Advancement Project (2014).
67. Kostyo et al. (2018), p. 6.
68. Kostyo et al. (2018). "We identify these as 'equity indicators' because they aim
    to open up and strengthen opportunities for learning. Because these indicators,
    along with the broader accountability indicators required under ESSA, must be
    reported for all student groups—by student race and ethnicity, economic disad-
    vantage, and language and special education status—they can reveal the dispari-
    ties that undermine opportunity so that schools may address the resulting gaps
    and needs" (p. v).
69. Kostyo et al. (2018), p. 6.
70. Rafa (2019), p. 4.

Chapter 5

1. Barber & Mourshed (2007).
2. L. Darling-Hammond & Oakes (2019); Noguera et al. (2015).
3. L. Darling-Hammond & Oakes (2019).
4. Guha et al. (2016).

5. Sutcher et al. (2016).
6. Cardichon et al. (2020).
7. Podolsky et al. (2019).
8. Clotfelter et al. (2007).
9. U.S. Department of Education (2013).
10. Carver-Thomas (2018).
11. Carver-Thomas (2018).
12. Baker et al. (2015).
13. Ingersoll et al. (2014); Ronfeldt et al. (2013).
14. Ronfeldt et al. (2013).
15. Carver-Thomas & Darling-Hammond (2017).
16. L. Darling-Hammond (2010); Oakes (2005).
17. M. Shapiro (1993), p. 89.
18. L. Darling-Hammond & Bransford (2005).
19. K. Carter & Doyle (1987).
20. L. Darling-Hammond & Oakes (2019).
21. L. Darling-Hammond, Cook-Harvey, et al. (2018); see also Snyder & Lit (2010).
22. L. Darling-Hammond, Cook-Harvey, et al. (2018).
23. U.S. Department of Education (2013); see also Jennings & Greenberg (2009).
24. L. Darling-Hammond (2010).
25. *Leandro v. State* (1997).
26. McColl (2020).
27. WestEd (2019).
28. *Horton v. Meskill* (1977).
29. *Sheff v. O'Neill* (1996).
30. Baron (1999).
31. Baron (1999), p. 28; L. Darling-Hammond (2010).
32. Boyd et al. (2008).
33. See L. Darling-Hammond (2008); L. Darling-Hammond & Oakes (2019); National Education Goals Panel (1998); National Research Council (2008).
34. L. Darling-Hammond et al. (2017).
35. L. Darling-Hammond (2014); Guha et al. (2016).
36. Podolsky et al. (2016).
37. Cannata et al. (2010); Cantrell et al. (2008); Zhu et al. (2019).

Chapter 6

1. Mehta (2014).
2. Gregory et al. (2010); Grissom & Redding (2016); Worrell et al. (2012).
3. L. Darling-Hammond et al. (2007).
4. Terman et al. (1922), pp. 27–28.
5. Pillsbury (1921), p. 71.
6. Oakes (2005).
7. L. Darling-Hammond & Adamson (2014).
8. Au (2007).
9. Noguera et al. (2015); see also U.S. Department of Education Office for Civil Rights (2016).
10. Kostyo et al. (2018).
11. Cook-Harvey et al. (2016).

12. Immordino-Yang et al. (2019).
13. Heckman & Masterov (2007); Reynolds et al. (2011).
14. Garcia et al. (2019).
15. Heckman (2011), pp. 31–32.
16. Isaacs (2012).
17. U.S. Department of Education (2013).
18. Bueno et al. (2010).
19. U.S. Department of Education (2013).
20. Barnett (2011).
21. Noguera et al. (2015), pp. 8–12; see also Friedlaender et al. (2014).
22. American Institutes of Research (2014).
23. Ancess et al. (2019); Cook-Harvey et al. (2020); Fine & Pryiomka (2020); Saunders et al. (2021); Thompson (2021).
24. Dee & Penner (2017); Bonilla et al. (2021).
25. Cabrera et al. (2014).
26. Hernández et al. (2019).
27. Leung et al. (2020).
28. Mickelson (2003).
29. Pootinath & Walsh (2011); George & Darling-Hammond (2021).
30. Cardichon & Darling-Hammond (2017).
31. Robinson (2021).
32. L. Darling-Hammond (2010).
33. L. Darling-Hammond & Adamson (2014).
34. Yuan & Le (2012).
35. L. Darling-Hammond (2007).
36. L. Darling-Hammond (2017).

References

Abbott v. Burke, 119 N.J. 287, 575 A.2d 359 (1990) (Abbott II).

Adams, D. W. (2020). *Education for extinction: American Indians and the boarding school experience, 1875–1928*. University Press of Kansas

Adisa-Farrar, T. (2021, March 30). How 600 years of environmental violence is still harming Black communities: The first transatlantic voyages were only the beginning. *Earth Justice*. https://earthjustice.org/blog/2021-march/overlooked-connections -between-black-injustice-and-environmentalism

Advancement Project, Padres and Jovenes Unidos, Southwest Youth Collaborative, and Children & Family Justice Center of Northwestern University School of Law. (2005). *Education on lockdown: The schoolhouse to jailhouse track*. https://www .njjn.org/uploads/digital-library/Education-on-Lockdown_Advancement-Project _2005.pdf

Advancement Project. (2014). *Restorative practices: Fostering healthy relationships & promoting positive discipline in schools*. https://advancementproject.org/resources /restorative-practices-fostering-healthy-relationships-promoting-positive-discipline -in-schools/

Advocates for Children and Youth. (2006, April). *School suspension: Effects and alternatives* (Issue Brief 3(6)). http://www.soros.org/sites/default/files/issuebrief _20060418.pdf

Amemiya, J., Mortenson, E., & Wang, M. (2020). Minor infractions are not minor: School infractions for minor misconduct may increase adolescents' defiant behavior and contribute to racial disparities in school discipline. *American Psychologist*, 75(1), 23–36. https://doi.apa.org/doi/10.1037/amp0000475

American Civil Liberties Union–Michigan. (2015, June 25). *Hard to swallow: Toxic water in a toxic system in Flint*. https://www.aclumich.org/en/news/hard-swallow -toxic-water-toxic-system-flint

American Civil Liberties Union–Michigan. (2020). *Special education in Flint*. https:// www.aclumich.org/en/cases/special-education-flint

American Institutes of Research. (2014). Study of deeper learning: Opportunities and outcomes. https://www.air.org/project/study-deeper-learning-opportunities-and -outcomes.

American Psychological Association Zero Tolerance Task Force. (2008). Are zero tolerance policies effective in the schools? An evidentiary review and recommendations. *American Psychologist*, 63(9), 852–862. https://doi.org/10.1037/0003 -066x.63.9.852

Ancess, J., Rogers, B., Duncan Grand, D., & Darling-Hammond, L. (2019). *Teaching the way students learn best: Lessons from Bronxdale High School*. Learning

Policy Institute. https://learningpolicyinstitute.org/product/social-and-emotional
-learning-case-study-bronxdale-report

Anderson, K., Ritter, G., & Zamarro, G. (2017). *Understanding a vicious cycle: Do out-of-school suspensions impact student test scores?* (EDRE Working Paper 2017-09). University of Arkansas Department of Education Reform. http://www.uaedreform.org/downloads/2017/03/understanding-a-vicious-cycle-do-out-of -school-suspensions-impact-student-test-scores.pdf

Anyon, J. (1997). *Ghetto schooling: A political economy of urban educational reform*. Teachers College Press.

Astor, R. A., Benbenishty, R., & Nuñez Estrada, J. (2009). School violence and theoretically atypical schools: The principal's centrality in orchestrating safe schools. *American Educational Research Journal, 46*, 423–461. https://doi.org/10.3102 /0002831208329598

Au, W. (2007). High-stakes testing and curricular control: A qualitative metasynthesis. *Educational Researcher, 36*(5), 258–267. https://doi.org/10.3102/0013189 X07306523

Augustine, C. H., Engberg, J., Grimm, G. E., Lee, E., Wang, E. L., Christianson, K., & Joseph, A. A. (2018). *Can restorative practices improve school climate and curb suspensions? An evaluation of the impact of restorative practices in a mid-sized urban school district*. RAND Corporation. https://www.rand.org/pubs/research _reports/RR2840.html

Bailey, M. J., & Duquette, N. J. (2014). How Johnson fought the war on poverty: The economics and politics of funding at the office of economic opportunity. *The Journal of Economic History, 74*(2), 351–388.

Baker, B., Sciarra, D. G., & Farrie, D. (2015). *Is school funding fair? A national report card, 4th edition*. Rutgers Education Law Center. http://www.schoolfundingfairness .org/is-school-funding-fair/reports

Baldwin, R. (2020, May 29). Covid, hysteresis, and the future of work. *VoxEU*. https://voxeu.org/article/covid-hysteresis-and-future-work

Balfanz, R., & Legters, N. E. (2004). Locating the dropout crisis: Which high schools produce the nation's dropouts? In Orfield, G. (Ed.), *Dropouts in America: Confronting the graduation rate crisis* (pp. 57–84). Harvard Education Press.

Barber, M., & Mourshed, M. (2007, September). *How the world's best-performing school systems come out on top*. McKinsey & Company Insights on Education. https://www.mckinsey.com/industries/education/our-insights/how-the-worlds -best-performing-school-systems-come-out-on-top

Barnett, S. (2011, September 22). *Preschool effectiveness and access*. Presented at the Equity and Excellence Commission.

Baron, J. B. (1999). *Exploring high and improving reading achievement in Connecticut*. National Educational Goals Panel.

Barton, P. E., Coley, R. J., & Goertz, M. E. (1991). *The state of inequality*. Educational Testing Service. https://www.ets.org/research/policy_research_reports /publications/report/1991/bbxo

Basch, C. E. (2011). Healthier students are better learners. *Journal of School Health, 81*(10), 591–592. https://doi.org/10.1111/j.1746-1561.2011.00631.x

Bean v. Southwestern Waste Management Corp., 482 F. Supp. 673 (S.D. Tex. 1979).

Berkowitz, R., Moore, H., Astor, R. A., & Benbenishty, R. (2016). A research synthesis of the associations between socioeconomic background, inequality, school climate, and academic achievement. *Review of Educational Research*, 87(2), 425–469. https://doi.org/10.3102/0034654316669821

Boccanfuso, C., & Kuhfeld, M. (2011). *Multiple responses, promising results: Evidence-based, nonpunitive alternatives to zero tolerance* (Research-to-Results Brief, Publication #2011-09). Child Trends. https://www.childtrends.org/wp-content/uploads/2011/03/Child_Trends-2011_03_01_RB_AltToZeroTolerance.pdf

Bonilla, S., Dee, T. S., & Penner, E. K. (2021). Ethnic studies increases longer-run academic engagement and attainment. *Proceedings of the National Academy of Sciences*, 118(37), e2026386118. https://doi.org/10.1073/pnas.2026386118

Boyd, D., Lankford, H., Loeb, S., Rockoff, J., & Wyckoff, J. (2008). The narrowing gap in New York City teacher qualifications and its implications for student achievement in high-poverty schools. *Journal of Policy Analysis and Management*, 27(4), 793–818. https://doi.org/10.1002/pam.20377

Braddock, J. H., II, & Gonzalez, A. D. C. (2010). Social isolation and social cohesion: The effects of K–12 neighborhood and school segregation on intergroup orientations. *Teachers College Record*, 112(6), 1631–1653. https://doi.org/10.1177/016146811011200606

Braddock, J. H., & McPartland, J. M. (1989). Social-psychological processes that perpetuate racial segregation: The relationship between school and employment desegregation. *Journal of Black Studies*, 19(3), 267–289. https://doi.org/10.1177/002193478901900301

Bridges, K. (2018). *Critical race theory: A primer* (Concepts and Insights). Foundation Press.

Bristol, T. J., & Martin-Fernandez, J. (2019). The added value of Latinx and Black teachers for Latinx and Black students: Implications for policy. *Policy Insights from the Behavioral and Brain Sciences*, 6(2), 147–153.

Brittain, J., Willis, L., & Cookson, P. W., Jr. (2019). *Sharing the wealth: How regional finance and desegregation plans can enhance educational equity.* Learning Policy Institute.

Brown v. Board of Education of Topeka, 347 U.S. 483 (1954).

Bueno, M., Darling-Hammond, L., & Gonzales, D. (2010). *A matter of degrees: Preparing teachers for the pre–K classroom.* Pew Center on the States.

Bullard, R. D. (1983). Solid waste sites and the Black Houston community. *Sociological inquiry*, 53(2–3), 273–288.

Bullard, R. D. (1996). *Unequal protection: Environmental justice and communities of color.* Sierra Club Books.

Bullard, R. D. (2004, October). *Environment and morality: Confronting environmental racism in the United States* [Programme Paper #8]. United Nations Research Institute for Social Development Identities, Conflict and Cohesion. Geneva, Switzerland.

Cabrera, N. L., Milem, J. F., Jaquette, O., & Marx, R. W. (2014). Missing the (student achievement) forest for all the (political) trees: Empiricism and the Mexican American studies controversy in Tucson. *American Education Research Journal*, 51(6), 1084–1118. https://doi.org/10.3102/0002831214553705

Cannata, M., McCory, R., Sykes, G., Anagnostopoulos, D., & Frank, K. (2010). Exploring the influence of National Board Certified Teachers in their schools and beyond. *Educational Administration Quarterly*, 46(4), 463–490.

Cantor, P., Osher, D., Berg, J., Steyer, L., & Rose, T. (2019). Malleability, plasticity, and individuality: How children learn and develop in context. *Applied Developmental Science*, 23(4), 307–337. https://doi.org/10.1080/10888691.2017.1398649

Cantrell, S., Fullerton, J., Kane, T. J., & Staiger, D. O. (2008). *National Board Certification and teacher effectiveness: Evidence from a random assignment experiment* (NBER Working Paper Series). National Bureau of Economic Research.

Cardichon, J., & Darling-Hammond, L. (2017). *Advancing educational equity for underserved youth: How new state accountability systems can support school inclusion and student success.* Learning Policy Institute. https://learningpolicyinstitute.org/product/advancing-educational-equity-underserved-youth-report

Cardichon, J., Darling-Hammond, L., Yang, M., Scott, C., Shields, P. M., & Burns, D. (2020). *Inequitable opportunity to learn: Student access to certified and experienced teachers.* Learning Policy Institute. https://learningpolicyinstitute.org/product/crdc-teacher-access-report

Carnevale, A. P., & Rose, S. J. (2015). The economy goes to college: The hidden promise of higher education in the post-industrial service economy. *Georgetown University Center on Education and the Workforce.*

Carnevale, A. P., Smith, N., Strohl, J. (2013). *Recovery: Job growth and education requirements through 2020.* Georgetown University Center on Education and the Workforce.

Carter, K., & Doyle, W. (1987). Teachers' knowledge structures and comprehension processes. In J. Calderhead (Ed.), *Exploring teacher thinking* (pp. 147–160). Cassell.

Carter, P., Bristol, T., & Darling-Hammond, K. (2016). *Authority, discipline, and the marginalization of youth in schools.* John W. Gardner Center for Youth and Their Communities. https://docs.google.com/document/d/1Jt-U5hQszmPoWBjRSgBz-agWt5gqy5o-I3IApd3Fmhs/pub

Carter, P. L., & Welner, K. G. (Eds.). (2013). *Closing the opportunity gap: What America must do to give every child an even chance.* Oxford University Press.

Carver-Thomas, D. (2018). *Diversifying the teaching profession: How to recruit and retain teachers of color.* Learning Policy Institute. https://doi.org/10.54300/559.310

Carver-Thomas, D., & Darling-Hammond, L. (2017). *Teacher turnover: Why it matters and what we can do about it.* Learning Policy Institute. https://doi.org/10.54300/454.278

Center for American Progress. (2011). *A conversation on civil rights in America.* https://www.americanprogress.org/issues/courts/news/2011/11/18/10692/the-enduring-importance-of-civil-rights/

Center on Poverty & Social Policy, Columbia University. (2022, February). *3.7 million more children in poverty in Jan 2022 without monthly Child Tax Credit (Policy Update).* https://www.povertycenter.columbia.edu/news-internal/monthly-poverty-january-2022

Centers for Disease Control and Prevention. (2021, April 6). *Violence prevention: Resources.* https://www.cdc.gov/violenceprevention/aces/resources.html

Centolanza, L. R. (1986). *The state and the schools: Consequences of curricular intervention, 1972–1980* [Doctoral dissertation]. Rutgers University.

Chen, Y., & Thomson, D. (2021, June 3). *Child poverty increased nationally during COVID, especially among Latino and Black children.* Child Trends. https://www

.childtrends.org/publications/child-poverty-increased-nationally-during-covid-especially-among-latino-and-black-children

Children's Defense Fund. (2021). *The state of America's children.* https://www.childrensdefense.org/state-of-americas-children/soac-2021-housing/

Christle, C. A., Jolivette, K., & Nelson, C. M. (2005). Breaking the school to prison pipeline: Identifying school risk and protective factors for youth delinquency. *Exceptionality, 13*(2), 69–88.

Clotfelter, C. T., Ladd, H. F., & Vigdor, J. L. (2007). *How and why do teacher credentials matter for student achievement?* (NBER Working Paper #12828). National Bureau of Economic Research. https://www.nber.org/papers/w12828

Cohen Milstein Sellers & Toll PLLC. (2021). *Flint water crisis class action litigation.* https://www.cohenmilstein.com/case-study/flint-water-crisis-class-action-litigation

Collaborative for Academic, Social, and Emotional Learning. (n.d.). *Fundamentals of SEL.* https://casel.org/fundamentals-of-sel

Comer, J. P., Haynes, N. M., Joyner, E. T., & Ben-Avie, M. (Eds.). (1996). *Rallying the whole village: The Comer process for reforming education.* Teachers College Press.

Comer, J. P., & Savo, C. (2009). *Focused on development: The Davis Street Interdistrict Magnet School in New Haven, Connecticut* [Video recording]. Comer School Development Program, Yale Child Study Center.

Contractor, D., & Staats, C. (2014). *Interventions to address racialized discipline disparities and school "push out."* Kirwan Institute. http://kirwaninstitute.osu.edu/wp-content/uploads/2014/05/ki-interventions.pdf

Cook-Harvey, C. M., Darling-Hammond, L., Lam, L., Mercer, C., & Roc, M. (2016). *Equity and ESSA: Leveraging educational opportunity through the Every Student Succeeds Act.* Learning Policy Institute. https://learningpolicyinstitute.org/product/equity-essa-report

Cook-Harvey, C. M., Flook, L., Efland, E., & Darling-Hammond, L. (2020). *Teaching for powerful learning: Lessons from Gateway Public Schools.* Learning Policy Institute. https://learningpolicyinstitute.org/product/social-and-emotional-learning-case-study-gateway-report;

Cookson, P. W., Jr., & Darling-Hammond, L. (2022). *Building school communities for children living in deep poverty.* Learning Policy Institute.

Craddock, A., Hecht, C., Poole, M. K., Vollmer, L., Flax, C., & Barrett, J. (2019). *Early adopters: State approaches to testing school drinking water for lead in the United States* [Research report]. Harvard T. H. Chan School of Public Health. https://www.hsph.harvard.edu/prc/projects/school-research/early-adopters

Cremin, L. A. (1970). *American education: The colonial experience 1607–1783.* Harper & Row.

Darling-Hammond, K. (2021). Dimensions of thriving: Learning from Black LGBTQ+/SGL moments, spaces, and practices. *Nonprofit Quarterly, Winter,* 20–29.

Darling-Hammond, K., Breland-Noble, A., Ginwright, S., Johns, D. J., & Norrington-Sands, K. (2020, September 12). *Public health disparities, including the crisis of Black youth suicide.* Presented at CAAASA's Virtual Annual Round-Up: Strengthening Equity Education Coalitions for African Americans [Symposium]. https://roundup.extendedsession.com

Darling-Hammond, L. (2001). Apartheid in American education: How opportunity is rationed to children of color in the United States. In T. Johnson, J. E. Boyden, & W. J. Pittz (Eds.), *Racial profiling and punishment in U.S. public schools* (pp. 39–44). Applied Research Center.

Darling-Hammond, L. (2007). Race, inequality, and educational accountability: The irony of "No Child Left Behind." *Race Ethnicity and Education, 10*(3), 245–260. https://doi.org/10.1080/13613320701503207

Darling-Hammond, L. (2008). Reshaping teaching policy, preparation, and practice: Influences of the National Board for Professional Teaching Standards. In H. Hattie & L. Ingvarson (Eds.), *Assessing teachers for professional certification: The National Board for Professional Teaching Standards* (pp. 25–54). Emerald Press.

Darling-Hammond, L. (2010). *The flat world and education: How America's commitment to equity will determine our future.* Teachers College Press.

Darling-Hammond, L. (2014). Strengthening clinical preparation: The Holy Grail of teacher education. *Peabody Journal of Education, 8*(4), 547–561. doi: 10.1080/0161956X.2014.939009

Darling-Hammond, L. (2017). *Developing and measuring higher order skills: Models for state performance assessment systems.* Council for Chief State School Officers and Learning Policy Institute. https://learningpolicyinstitute.org/sites/default/files/product-files/Models_State_Performance_Assessment_Systems_REPORT.pdf

Darling-Hammond, L. (2018). *Education and the path to one nation, indivisible.* Learning Policy Institute. https://learningpolicyinstitute.org/product/education-path-one-nation-indivisible-brief

Darling-Hammond, L. (2019). *Investing for student success: Lessons from state school finance reforms.* Learning Policy Institute. https://learningpolicyinstitute.org/product/investing-student-success-school-finance-reforms-report

Darling-Hammond, L., & Adamson, F. (Eds.) (2014). *Beyond the bubble test: How performance assessments support 21st century learning.* Jossey-Bass.

Darling-Hammond, L., & Bransford, J. (Eds.). (2005). *Preparing teachers for a changing world: What teachers should learn and be able to do.* Jossey-Bass.

Darling-Hammond, L., Burns, D., Campbell, C., Goodwin, A. L., Hamerness, K., Low, E., McIntire, A., Sato, M., & Zeichner, K. (2017). *Empowered educators; How high-perfoming systems shape teaching quality around the world.* Jossey-Bass.

Darling-Hammond, L., & Cook-Harvey, C. M. (2018). *Educating the whole child: Improving school climate to support student success.* Learning Policy Institute. https://doi.org/10.54300/145.655

Darling-Hammond, L., Cook-Harvey, C. M., Flook, L., Gardner, M., & Melnick, H. (2018). *With the whole child in mind: Insights from the Comer School Development Program.* ASCD.

Darling-Hammond, L., Flook, L., Cook-Harvey, C., Barron, B., & Osher, D. (2019). Implications for educational practice of the science of learning and development. *Applied Developmental Science, 24*(2), 97–140. https://doi.org/10.1080/10888691.2018.1537791

Darling-Hammond, L., Friedlaender, D., & Snyder, J. (2014a). *Student-centered schools: Policy supports for closing the opportunity gap.* Stanford Center for Opportunity Policy in Education.

Darling-Hammond, L., & Oakes, J. (2019). *Preparing teachers for deeper learning.* Harvard Education Press.

Darling-Hammond, L., Williamson, J., & Hyler, M. (2007). Securing the right to learn: The quest for an empowering curriculum for African American citizens. *Journal of Negro Education, 76*(3), 281–296.

Darling-Hammond, L., Zielezinski, M. B., & Goldman, S. (2014b). *Using technology to support at-risk students' learning.* Alliance for Excellent Education.

Darling-Hammond, S. (forthcoming). *The power of restorative practices.* Learning Policy Institute.

Davis, M. M., Kolb, C., Reynolds, L., Rothstein, E., & Sikkema, K. (2016, March 21). *Flint Water Advisory Task Force final report.* Office of the Governor, State of Michigan.

Dee, T., & Penner, E. K. (2017). The causal effects of cultural relevance: Evidence from an ethnic studies curriculum. *American Educational Research Journal, 54*(1), 127–166. https://doi.org/10.3102/0002831216677002

D.R. v. Michigan Department of Education, Case No. 16-13694 (E.D. Mich. Sep. 29, 2017).

Downes, T. A., Zabel, J., & Ansel, D. (2009). *Incomplete grade: Massachusetts education reform at 15.* MassINC.

Durlak, J. A., Weissberg, R. P., Dymnicki, A. B., Taylor, R. D., & Schellinger, K. B. (2011). The impact of enhancing students' social and emotional learning: A meta-analysis of school-based universal interventions. *Child Development, 82*(1), 405–432. https://doi.org/10.1111/j.1467-8624.2010.01564.x

Dweck, C. S., & Yeager, D. S. (2019). Mindsets: A view from two eras. *Perspectives on Psychological Science, 14*(3), 481–496.

Educational Services for Children Affected by Lead Expert Panel. (2015). *Educational interventions for children affected by lead.* U.S. Department of Health and Human Services. https://www.cdc.gov/nceh/lead/publications/educational_interventions_children_affected_by_lead.pdf

Ekono, M., Yang, J., & Smith, S. (2016). *Young children in deep poverty.* National Center for Children in Poverty, Mailman School of Public Health, Columbia University. https://www.nccp.org/wp-content/uploads/2016/01/text_1133.pdf

Fabelo, T., Thompson, M., Plotkin, M., Carmichael, D., Marchbanks, M., III, & Booth, E. (2011). *Breaking schools' rules: A statewide study of how school discipline relates to students' success and juvenile justice involvement.* The Council of State Governments Justice Center & Public Policy Research Institute. https://csgjusticecenter.org/wp-content/uploads/2020/01/Breaking_Schools_Rules_Report_Final.pdf

Farrie, D., & Sciarra, D. G. (2021). *Making the grade 2021: How fair is school funding in your state?* Education Law Center. https://edlawcenter.org/research/making-the-grade-2021.html

Felton, E. (2017, September 6). The Department of Justice is overseeing the resegregation of American schools. *The Nation.* https://www.thenation.com/article/archive/the-department-of-justice-is-overseeing-the-resegregation-of-american-schools

Fenning, P., & Rose, J. (2007). Overrepresentation of African American students in exclusionary discipline: The role of school policy. *Urban Education, 42*(6), 536–559. https://doi.org/10.1177/0042085907305039

Fine, M., & Pryiomka, K. (2020). *Assessing college readiness through authentic student work: How the City University of New York and the New York Performance*

Standards Consortium are collaborating toward equity. Learning Policy Institute. https://learningpolicyinstitute.org/product/assessing-college-readiness-authentic-student-work-report

Fishman, N., & Hack, D. (2012). School-based youth courts: Creating a restorative justice alternative to traditional school disciplinary responses. In *Keeping kids in school and out of courts: A collection of reports to the National Leadership Summit on School–Justice Partnerships* (pp. 155–168). New York State Permanent Judicial Commission on Justice for Children. https://www.nycourts.gov/ip/justiceforchildren/PDF/Collection-of-Reports.pdf

Fortner, S. (2021). Erasing the redline: Addressing lead poisoning and environmental racism through research, education, and advocacy. *Liberal Education, 107*(1). https://www.aacu.org/article/erasing-the-redline

Fox, L., Garfinkel, I., Kaushal, N., Waldfogel, J., & Wimer, C. (2014). *Waging war on poverty: Historical trends in poverty using the supplemental poverty measure* (Working Paper No. 19789). National Bureau of Economic Research. https://www.nber.org/papers/w19789

Franke, H. A. (2014). Toxic stress: Effects, prevention and treatment. *Children, 1*(3), 390–402. https://doi.org/10.3390/children1030390

Frankenberg, E., Hawley, G., Ee, J., & Orfield, G. (2017). *Southern schools: More than a half-century after the civil rights revolution* (pp. 1–18). Civil Rights Project.

Friedlaender, D. (2014). *Student-centered learning: Dozier-Libbey Medical High School*. Stanford Center for Opportunity Policy in Education.

Friedlaender, D., Burns, D., Lewis-Charp, H., Cook-Harvey, C. M., Zheng, X., & Darling-Hammond, L. (2014). *Student-centered schools: Closing the opportunity gap*. Stanford Center for Opportunity Policy in Education.

Fronius, T., Darling-Hammond, S., Persson, H., Guckenburg, S., Hurley, N., & Petrosino, A. (2019). *Restorative justice in U.S. schools: An updated research review*. WestEd. https://files.eric.ed.gov/fulltext/ED595733.pdf

Garcia, J. L., Heckman, J. J., Leaf, D. E., & Prados, M. J. (2019). *Quantifying the life-cycle benefits of a prototypical early childhood program*. National Bureau of Economic Research. https://heckmanequation.org/www/assets/2017/01/w23479.pdf

Garza, F. (2021, February 11). America's dirty divide: How environmental racism leaves the vulnerable behind. *The Guardian*. https://www.theguardian.com/us-news/2021/feb/11/environmental-racism-americas-dirty-divide

George, J., & Darling-Hammond, L. (2019). *The federal role and school integration: Brown's promise and present challenges*. Learning Policy Institute. https://learningpolicyinstitute.org/product/federal-role-school-integration-browns-promise-report

George, J., & Darling-Hammond, L. (2021). *Advancing integration and equity through magnet schools*. Learning Policy Institute. https://learningpolicyinstitute.org/product/advancing-integration-equity-magnet-schools-report

Gilliam, W. (2016). *Early childhood suspensions and expulsions undermine our nation's most promising agent of opportunity and social justice* [Issue brief]. Yale Child Study Center. https://themoriahgroup.com/wp-content/uploads/2018/05/early-childhood-expulsions-and-suspensions.pdf

Gilliam, W. S., Maupin, A. N., Reyes, C. R., Accavitti, M., & Shic, F. (2016). *Do early educators' implicit biases regarding sex and race relate to behavior expectations and recommendations of preschool expulsions and suspensions?* [Research study brief]. Yale Child Study Center, Yale University.

Green, E. L. (2019, November 6). Flint's children suffer in class after years of drinking the lead-poisoned water. *The New York Times.* https://www.nytimes.com/2019/11/06/us/politics/flint-michigan-schools.html

Gregory, A., Skiba, R. J., & Noguera, P. A. (2010). The achievement gap and the discipline gap: Two sides of the same coin? *Educational Researcher, 39*(1), 59–68. https://doi.org/10.3102/0013189X09357621

Grissom, J. A., & Redding, C. (2016). Discretion and disproportionality: Explaining the underrepresentation of high-achieving students of color in gifted programs. *AERA Open, 2*(1). https://doi.org/10.1177/2332858415622175

Guha, R., Hyler, M. E., & Darling-Hammond, L. (2016). *The teacher residency: An innovative model for preparing teachers.* Learning Policy Institute.

Guryan, J. (2001). *Does money matter? Regression-discontinuity estimates from education finance reform in Massachusetts* (NBER Working Paper No. 8269). National Bureau of Economic Research.

Guyette, C. (2017, April 19). A deep dive into the source of Flint's water crisis. *Detroit Metro Times.* https://www.metrotimes.com/detroit/a-deep-dive-into-the-source-of-flints-water-crisis/Content?oid=3399011

Guyette, C. (2018, April 25). The Flint water crisis isn't over. *ACLU Blog.* https://www.aclu.org/blog/racial-justice/race-and-economic-justice/flint-water-crisis-isnt-over

Hallinan, M. (1998). Diversity effects on student outcomes: Social science evidence. *Ohio State Law Journal, 59,* 733–754.

Hanna-Attisha, M., LaChance, J., Sadler, R. C., & Schnepp, A. C. (2016). Elevated blood lead levels in children associated with the Flint drinking water crisis: A spatial analysis of risk and public health response. *American Journal of Public Health, 106*(2), 283–290. https://doi.org/10.2105/AJPH.2015.303003

Hanushek, E. (2003). The structure of analysis and argument in plaintiff expert reports for *Williams v. State of California,* p. 4. http://www.decentschools.org/expert_reports/hanushek_report.pdf

Harry, B., & Klingner, J. (2006). *Why are so many minority students in special education? Understanding race and disability in schools.* Teachers College Press.

Heckman, J. J. (2011). The economics of inequality, the value of early childhood education. *The American Educator, 35*(1), 31–35.

Heckman, J. J., & Masterov, D. V. (2007). The productivity argument for investing in young children. *Review of Agricultural Economics, 29*(3), 446–493.

Hernández, L. E., Darling-Hammond, L., Adams, J., & Bradley, K. (with Duncan Grand, D., Roc, M., & Ross, P.). (2019). *Deeper learning networks: Taking student-centered learning and equity to scale.* Learning Policy Institute. https://learningpolicyinstitute.org/product/deeper-learning-networks-report

Hewlett Foundation. (2013). *Deeper learning competencies.* http://www.hewlett.org/library/hewlett-foundation-publication/deeper-learning-defined

Hoffman, J. S., Shandas, V., & Pendleton, N. (2020). The effects of historical housing policies on resident exposure to intra-urban heat: A study of 108 US urban areas. *Climate, 8*(1), 12. https://doi.org/10.3390/cli8010012

Horner, R. H., Sugai, G., Smolkowski, K., Eber, L., Nakasato, J., Todd, A. W., & Esperanza, J. (2009). A randomized, wait-list controlled effectiveness trial assessing school-wide positive behavior support in elementary schools. *Journal of Positive Behavior Interventions, 11,* 133–144. https://doi.org/10.1177/1098300709332067

Horton v. Meskill, 172 Conn. 615, 376 A.2d 359 (Conn. 1977).

Hurtado, S. (2005). The next generation of diversity and intergroup relations research. *Journal of Social Issues, 61*(3), 595–610. https://doi.org/10.1111/j.1540-4560 .2005.00422.x

Immordino-Yang, M. H., Darling-Hammond, L., & Krone, C. R. (2019). Nurturing nature: How brain development is inherently social and emotional, and what this means for education. *Educational Psychologist, 54*(3), 185–204. https://doi.org /10.1080/00461520.2019.1633924

Infrastructure Investment and Jobs Act of 2021, H.R. 3684, 117 Cong., 1st Sess. (2021). https://www.congress.gov/117/bills/hr3684/BILLS-117hr3684enr.pdf

Ingersoll, R., Merrill, L., & May, H. (2014). *What are the effects of teacher education preparation on beginning teacher attrition?* Consortium for Policy Research in Education, University of Pennsylvania.

Isaacs, J. B. (2012). *Starting school at a disadvantage: The school readiness of poor children.* Brookings Institution. https://www.brookings.edu/wp-content/uploads /2016/06/0319_school_disadvantage_isaacs.pdf

Jackson, C. K., Johnson, R. C., & Persico, C. (2014). *The effect of school finance reforms on the distribution of spending, academic achievement and adult outcomes* (NBER Working Paper 20118). National Bureau of Economic Research. https:// www.nber.org/papers/w20118

Jennings, P. A., & Greenberg, M. T. (2009). The prosocial classroom: Teacher social and emotional competence in relation to student and classroom outcomes. *Review of Educational Research, 79*(1), 491–525. https://doi.org/10.3102/0034654308325693

Johnson, R. C. (2011). *Long-run impacts of school desegregation and school quality on adult attainments* [NBER Working Paper #16664]. National Bureau of Economic Research.

Johnson, R. C. (2019). *Children of the dream: Why school integration works.* Basic Books.

Joyner, E. T., Comer, J. P., & Ben-Avie, M. (2004). *Comer schools in action: The 3-volume field guide.* Corwin Press.

Kelly, S. (2010). A crisis of authority in predominantly Black schools? *Teachers College Record, 112*(5), 1247–1274. https://doi.org/10.1177/016146811011200501

Kim, C. Y., Losen, D. J., & Hewitt, D. T. (2010). *The school-to-prison pipeline: Structuring legal reform.* New York University Press.

Klevan, S. (2021). *Building a positive school climate through restorative practices.* Learning Policy Institute. https://doi.org/10.54300/178.861

Konold, T., Cornell, D., Shukla, K., & Huang, F. (2017). Racial/ethnic differences in perceptions of school climate and its association with student engagement and peer aggression. *Journal of Youth and Adolescence, 46*(6), 1289–1303. https:// doi.org/10.1007/s10964-016-0576-1

Kosciw, J. G., Greytak, E. A., Zongrone, A. D., Clark, C. M., & Truong, N. L. (2017). *The 2017 National School Climate Survey: The experiences of lesbian, gay, bisexual, transgender, and queer youth in our nation's schools.* GLSEN.

Kostyo, S., Cardichon, J., & Darling-Hammond, L. (2018). *Making ESSA's equity promise real: State strategies to close the opportunity gap.* Learning Policy Institute. https://learningpolicyinstitute.org/product/essa-equity-promise

Krivo, L. J., Peterson, R. D., & Kuhl, D. C. (2009). Segregation, racial structure, and neighborhood violent crime. *American Journal of Sociology, 114*(6), 1765–1802. https://doi.org/10.1086/597285

Kurlaender, M., & Yun, J. T. (2007). Measuring school racial composition and student outcomes in a multiracial society. *American Journal of Education, 113*(2), 213–242. https://doi.org/10.1086/510166

Lakhani, N. (2020, January 13). 'Heat islands': Racist housing policies in US linked to deadly heatwave exposure. *The Guardian*. https://www.theguardian.com/society/2020/jan/13/racist-housing-policies-us-deadly-heatwaves-exposure-study

Lassen, S. R., Steele, M. M., & Sailor, W. (2006). The relationship of school-wide positive behavior support to academic achievement in an urban middle school. *Psychology in the Schools, 43*(6), 701–712. https://doi.org/10.1002/pits.20177

Leandro v. State, 488 S.E.2d 249 (N.C. 1997).

Learning Policy Institute and Turnaround for Children. (2021). *Design principles for schools: Putting the science of learning and development into action.* https://k12.designprinciples.org

Leung, M., Cardichon, J., Scott, C., & Darling-Hammond, L. (2020). *Inequitable opportunity to learn: Access to advanced mathematics and science courses.* Learning Policy Institute. https://learningpolicyinstitute.org/product/crdc-course-access-report

Leung, M., Scott, C., Losen, D., & Campoli, A. (2022). *Inequitable opportunity to learn: Out of school suspensions.* Learning Policy Institute.

Linn, R., & Welner, K. (2007). *Race-conscious policies for assigning students to schools: Social science research and the Supreme Court cases.* National Academy of Education.

Locke, D. H., Hall, B., Grove, J. M., Pickett, S. T., Ogden, L. A., Aoki, C., Boone, C. G., & O'Neil-Dunne, J. P. (2021). Residential housing segregation and urban tree canopy in 37 US cities. *npj Urban Sustainability, 1*(1), 15. https://doi.org/10.1038/s42949-021-00022-0

Lombardi, K., Buford, T., & Greene, R. (2015). *Environmental racism persists, and the EPA is one reason why.* Center for Public Integrity. https://publicintegrity.org/environment/environmental-racism-persists-and-the-epa-is-one-reason-why/

Losen, D. J., & Gillespie, J. (2012). *Opportunities suspended: The disparate impact of disciplinary exclusion from school.* Civil Rights Project/Proyecto Derechos Civiles.

Losen, D. J., Hodson, C. L., Ee, J., & Martinez, T. (2014). Disturbing inequities: Exploring the relationship between racial disparities in special education identification and discipline. *Journal of Applied Research on Children, 5*(2), 15

Loveless, T. (2017). *The 2017 Brown Center Report on American education: How well are students learning? Part III: Race and school suspensions.* Brookings Institution. https://www.brookings.edu/research/2017-brown-center-report-part-iii-race-and-school-suspensions/

MacFarlane, K., & Woolfson, L. M. (2013). Teacher attitudes and behavior toward the inclusion of children with social, emotional and behavioral difficulties in mainstream schools: An application of the theory of planned behavior. *Teaching and Teacher Education, 29*, 46–52. https://doi.org/10.1016/j.tate.2012.08.006

Maier, A, Daniel, J., Oakes, J. & Lam, L. (2017). *Community schools as an effective school improvement strategy: A review of the evidence.* Learning Policy Institute.

Marshall, B., & Ruane, K. (2021, April 28). How broadband access advances systemic equality. *American Civil Liberties Union News.* https://www.aclu.org/news/privacy-technology/how-broadband-access-hinders-systemic-equality-and-deepens-the-digital-divide/

Mathewson, T. G. (2020, October 31). New data: Even within the same district some wealthy schools get millions more than poor ones. *The Hechinger Report.* https:// hechingerreport.org/new-data-even-within-the-same-district-some-wealthy -schools-get-millions-more-than-poor-ones/

McColl, N. (2020, February 17). Everything you need to know about the Leandro litigation. *EdNC.* https://www.ednc.org/leandro-litigation/

McUsic, M. (1991). The use of education clauses in school finance reform litigation. *Harvard Journal on Legislation, 28*(2), 307–340.

Mehta, J. (2014, June 20). Deeper learning has a race problem. *Education Week.* https://www.edweek.org/leadership/opinion-deeper-learning-has-a-race-problem /2014/06

Melnick, H., Cook-Harvey, C. M., & Darling-Hammond, L. (2017). *Encouraging social and emotional learning in the context of new accountability.* Learning Policy Institute. https://learningpolicyinstitute.org/product/encouraging-social-emotional -learning-new-accountability-report

Michigan in the World and the Environmental Justice HistoryLab. (2017). *Give Earth a chance* [Online exhibition]. https://michiganintheworld.history.lsa.umich.edu /environmentalism/exhibits/show/main_exhibit/pollution_politics/national--air -quality

Mickelson, R. A. (2003). The academic consequences of desegregation and segregation: Evidence from the Charlotte-Mecklenburg schools. *North Carolina Law Review, 81*(4), 1513–1562.

Mickelson, R. A. (2008). Twenty-first century social science research on school racial diversity and educational outcomes. *Ohio State Law Journal, 69,* 1173–1228.

Mickelson, R. A. (2016). *School integration and K–12 outcomes: An updated quick synthesis of the social science evidence.* National Coalition on School Diversity. https://www.school-diversity.org/pdf/DiversityResearchBriefNo5.pdf

Mickelson, R. A., & Bottia, M. (2010). Integrated education and mathematics outcomes: A synthesis of social science research. *North Carolina Law Review, 88*(3), 993–1090.

Mickelson, R. A., & Nkomo, M. (2012). Integrated schooling, life course outcomes, and social cohesion in multiethnic democratic societies. *Review of Research in Education, 36*(1), 197–238. https://doi.org/10.3102/0091732X11422667

Milam, A. J., Furr-Holden, C. D. M., & Leaf, P. J. (2010). Perceived school and neighborhood safety, neighborhood violence and academic achievement in urban school children. *The Urban Review, 42*(5), 458–467. https://doi.org/10.1007 /s11256-010-0165-7

Milman, O. (2018, December 20). Robert Bullard: 'Environmental justice isn't just slang, it's real.' *The Guardian.* https://www.theguardian.com/commentisfree/2018 /dec/20/robert-bullard-interview-environmental-justice-civil-rights-movement

Mitchell, C. (2019, August 26). In Flint, schools overwhelmed by special education needs in aftermath of lead crisis. *Education Week.* https://www.edweek.org /teaching-learning/in-flint-schools-overwhelmed-by-special-ed-needs-in-aftermath -of-lead-crisis/2019/08

Morris, E. W., & Perry, B. L. (2016). The punishment gap: School suspension and racial disparities in achievement. *Social Problems, 63*(1), 68–86. https://doi.org /10.1093/socpro/spv026

Nation's Report Card (n.d.). *National assessment of educational progress long-term trend assessment results: Reading.* https://www.nationsreportcard.gov/ltt/reading/student-group-scores/?age=13

National Education Goals Panel. (1998). *The National Education Goals report: Building a nation of learners.* Author.

National Research Council. (2008). *Assessing accomplished teaching: Advanced-level certification programs.* National Academies Press.

National School Climate Center. (n.d.). *What is school climate?* https://www.schoolclimate.org/about/our-approach/what-is-school-climate

National Scientific Council on the Developing Child. (2010). *Persistent fear and anxiety can affect young children's learning and development* (Working Paper No. 9). https://developingchild.harvard.edu/resources/persistent-fear-and-anxiety-can-affect-young-childrens-learning-and-development/.

Nelson, L. (2016, February 15). The Flint water crisis, explained. *Vox.* https://www.vox.com/2016/2/15/10991626/flint-water-crisis

Nguyen-Hoang, P., & Yinger, J. (2014). Education finance reform, local behavior, and student performance in Massachusetts. *Journal of Education Finance, 39,* 297–322.

Noguera, P., Darling-Hammond, L., & Friedlaender, D. (2015). *Equal opportunity for deeper learning. Students at the center* (Deeper Learning Research Series). Jobs for the Future.

Oakes, J. (2005). *Keeping track: How schools structure inequality* (2nd ed.). Yale University Press.

Office of the Assistant Secretary for Planning and Evaluation. (2022). *HHS poverty guidelines.* U.S. Department of Health and Human Services. https://aspe.hhs.gov/topics/poverty-economic-mobility/poverty-guidelines

Office of Special Education Programs Technical Assistance Center, Positive Behavioral Interventions & Supports. (2015). *PBIS implementation blueprint.* https://www.pbis.org/resource/pbis-implementation-blueprint-part-1

Opening Doors, Expanding Opportunities, 81 (240) Fed. Reg. 90343 (December 14, 2016) (to be codified at 34 CFR 75.127–129).

Orfield, G., Ee, J., Frankenberg, E., & Siegel-Hawley, G. (2016). *Brown at 62: School segregation by race, poverty and state.* Civil Rights Project. https://www.civilrightsproject.ucla.edu/research/k-12-education/integration-and-diversity/brown-at-62-school-segregation-by-race-poverty-and-state/Brown-at-62-final-corrected-2.pdf

Osher, D., Bear, G. G., Sprague, J. R., & Doyle, W. (2010). How can we improve school discipline? *Educational Researcher, 39*(1), 48–58. https://doi.org/10.3102/0013189X09357618

Page, S. (2008). *The difference: How the power of diversity creates better groups, firms, schools, and societies.* Princeton University Press.

Parents Involved in Cmty. Schs. v. Seattle Sch. Dist. No. 1, 551 U.S. 701, 723 (2007).

Parolin, Z., Collyer, S., Curran, M. A., & Wimer, C. (2021). *The potential poverty reduction effect of the American Rescue Plan* (Fact sheet). Center on Poverty and Social Policy, Columbia University. https://www.povertycenter.columbia.edu/news-internal/2021/presidential-policy/biden-economic-relief-proposal-poverty-impact

Pastor, M., & Morello-Frosch, R. (2018). Gaps matter: Environment, health, and social equity. *Generations: Journal of the American Society on Aging, 42*(2), 28–33.

Pastor, M., Sadd, J. L., & Morello-Frosch, R. (2004). Reading, writing, and toxics: Children's health, academic performance, and environmental justice in Los Angeles. *Environment and Planning C: Politics and Space, 22*(2), 271–290. https://doi.org/10.1068/c009r

Payton, J., Weissberg, R. P., Durlak, J. A., Dymnicki, A. B., Taylor, R. D., Schellinger, K. B., & Pachan, M. (2008). *The positive impact of social and emotional learning for kindergarten to eighth-grade students: Findings from three scientific reviews* [Technical report]. Collaborative for Academic, Social, and Emotional Learning.

Pillsbury, W. B. (1921). Selection—An unnoticed function of education. *Scientific Monthly, 12*(1), 62–74.

Podolsky, A., Darling-Hammond, L., Doss, C., & Reardon, S. (2019). *California's positive outliers: Districts beating the odds.* Learning Policy Institute. https://learningpolicyinstitute.org/product/positive-outliers-districts-beating-odds-report

Podolsky, A., Kini, T., Bishop, J., & Darling-Hammond, L. (2016). *Solving the teacher shortage: How to attract and retain excellent educators.* Learning Policy Institute. https://doi.org/10.54300/262.960

Pootinath, P., & Walsh, N. (2011). *Desegregated schools with segregated classrooms: The reality of racialized tracking at magnet schools.* Cities, Suburbs & Schools Project at Trinity College. https://commons.trincoll.edu/cssp/2011/12/06/pornpat-and-nathan-temporary-title/

Prucha, F. P. (2014). *The Great Father: The United States government and the American Indians.* University of Nebraska Press.

Pulido, L. (2000). Rethinking environmental racism: White privilege and urban development in Southern California. *Annals of the Association of American Geographers, 90*(1), 12–40. https://doi.org/10.1111/0004-5608.00182

Rafa, A. (2019). *Policy analysis: The status of school discipline in state policy.* Education Commission of the States.

Raffaele Mendez, L. M., & Knoff, H. M. (2003). Who gets suspended from school and why: A demographic analysis of schools and disciplinary infractions in a large school district. *Education and Treatment of Children, 26*(1), 30–51.

Rausch, M. K., Skiba, R. J., & Simmons, A. B. (2005, April). *The academic cost of discipline: The relationship between suspension/expulsion and school achievement.* Presented at the Annual Meeting of the American Educational Research Association, Montreal, Canada. https://pdfs.semanticscholar.org/9d53/05902807041b69543b7e2d864d9e68fc56e4.pdf

Reardon, S., Grewal, E. T., Kalogrides, D., & Greenberg, E. (2012). *Brown* fades: The end of court-ordered school desegregation and the resegregation of American public schools. *Journal of Policy Analysis and Management, 31*(4), 876–904.

Redfield, S. E., & Nance, J. P. (2016). *The American Bar Association Joint Task Force on Reversing the School-to-Prison Pipeline preliminary report.* American Bar Association Coalition on Racial and Ethnic Justice, Criminal Justice Section, and Council for Racial & Ethnic Diversity in the Educational Pipeline. https://scholarship.law.ufl.edu/facultypub/750/

Reynolds, A. J., Temple, J. A., Ou, S., Arteaga, I. A., & White, B. A. B. (2011). School-based early childhood education and age-28 well-being: Effects by timing, dosage, and subgroups. *Science, 333*(6040), 360–364. https://doi.org/10.1126/science.1203618

Richardson, N., & Feldman, J. (2014). *Student-centered learning: Life Academy of Health and Bioscience.* Stanford Center for Opportunity Policy in Education.

Ringquist, E. J. (2005). Assessing evidence of environmental inequities: A meta-analysis. *Journal of Policy Analysis and Management, 24*(2), 223–247. https://doi.org/10.1002/pam.20088

Robinson, K. J. (2021). *Protecting education as a civil right: Remedying racial discrimination and ensuring a high-quality education.* Learning Policy Institute. https://doi.org/10.54300/407.455

Roc, M., Ross, P., & Hernández, L. E. (2019). *Internationals Network for Public Schools: A deeper learning approach to supporting English learners.* Learning Policy Institute

Ronfeldt, M., Loeb, S., & Wyckoff, J. (2013). How teacher turnover harms student achievement. *American Educational Research Journal, 50*(1), 4–36.

Rothstein, R. (2004). *Class and schools: Using social, economic, and educational reform to close the Black–White achievement gap.* Economic Policy Institute.

Rothstein, R. (2017). *The color of law: A forgotten history of how our government segregated America.* Liveright Publishing.

Rubinkam, M. (2021, December 17). EPA releases $1B to clean up toxic waste sites in 24 states. *AP News.* https://apnews.com/article/joe-biden-environment-and-nature-environment-48cedbeea19e33329d65f34d3aae58ed

Ruckart, P. Z., Ettinger, A. S., Hanna-Attisha, M., Jones, N., Davis, S. I., & Breysse, P. N. (2019). The Flint water crisis: A coordinated public health emergency response and recovery initiative. *Journal of Public Health Management and Practice, 25*(Suppl. 1), S84–S90. https://doi.org/10.1097/PHH.0000000000000871

San Antonio Independent School District v. Rodriguez, 411 U.S. 1 1973.

Santos, T., Medina, C., & Gruberg, S. (2021, March 15). *What you need to know about the Equality Act.* Center for American Progress. https://www.americanprogress.org/issues/lgbtq-rights/reports/2021/03/15/497158/need-know-equality-act

Saunders, M., Martínez, L., Flook, L., & Hernández, L. E. (2021). *Social Justice Humanitas Academy: A community school approach to whole child education.* Learning Policy Institute. https://learningpolicyinstitute.org/product/social-and-emotional-learning-case-study-humanitas-report

Schiff, M., & Bazemore, G. (2012). "Whose kids are these?" Juvenile justice and education partnerships using restorative justice to end the "School-to-Prison Pipeline." In *Keeping kids in school and out of courts: A collection of reports to the National Leadership Summit on School–Justice Partnerships* (pp. 68–82). New York State Permanent Judicial Commission on Justice for Children. https://www.nycourts.gov/ip/justiceforchildren/PDF/Collection-of-Reports.pdf

Schofield, J. W. (2001). Maximizing the benefits of a diverse student body: Lessons from school desegregation research. In G. Orfield (Ed.), *Diversity challenged* (pp. 99–110). Harvard Education Publishing Group.

Schott Foundation for Public Education, Advancement Project, American Federation of Teachers, & National Education Association. (2014). *Restorative practices: Fostering healthy relationships and promoting positive discipline in schools.* http://schottfoundation.org/sites/default/files/restorative-practices-guide.pdf

Schwartz, H. (2010). *Housing policy is school policy: Economically integrative housing promotes academic success in Montgomery County, Maryland.* Century Foundation.

SCOPE. (2014). *Student-centered learning: How four schools are closing the opportunity gap*. Stanford Center for Opportunity Policy in Education. http://edpolicy.stanford.edu.

Seligman, B., Kress, D., Winfrey, W., Feranil, I., & Agarwal, K. (1997). *Reproductive health and human capital: A framework for expanding policy dialogue*. The Futures Group International, POLICY Project

Shaefer, H. L., Edin, K., & Nelson, T. (n.d.). *Understanding communities of deep disadvantage: An introduction*. Poverty Solutions, University of Michigan. http://sites.fordschool.umich.edu/poverty2021/files/2021/03/Communities-of-Deep-Disadvantage-introduction-1-29-20-2.pdf

Shapiro, M. (1993). *Who will teach for America?* Farragut Publishing.

Shapiro, T. M. (2017). Toxic inequality: How America's wealth gap destroys mobility, deepens the racial divide, and threatens our future. Basic Books.

Sheff v. O'Neill, 238 Conn. 1, 678 A.2d 1267 (Conn. 1996).

Simonsen, B., Freeman, J., Goodman, S., Mitchell, B., Swain-Bradway, J., Flannery, B., & Putman, B. (2015). *Supporting and responding to behavior: Evidence-based classroom strategies for teachers*. Office of Special Education Programs. https://osepideasthatwork.org/sites/default/files/ClassroomPBIS_508.pdf

Skiba, R. J., Michael, R. S., Nardo, A. C., & Peterson, R. L. (2002). The color of discipline: Sources of racial and gender disproportionality in school punishment. *The Urban Review, 34*, 317–342. https://doi.org/10.1023/A:1021320817372

Skiba, R. J., & Sprague, J. (2008). Safety without suspensions. *Safety, 66*(1), 38–43.

Skiba, R. J., & Williams, N. T. (2014). *Are Black kids worse? Myths and facts about racial differences in behavior*. The Equity Project at Indiana University.

Smith, J. P. (1999). Healthy bodies and thick wallets: The dual relation between health and economic status. *Journal of Economic Perspectives, 13*(2), 145–166. https://doi.org/10.1257/jep.13.2.145

Snyder, J., & Lit, I. (2010). *Principles and exemplars for integrating developmental sciences knowledge into educator preparation*. National Council for Accreditation of Teacher Education.

Steinberg, M. P., Allensworth, E., & Johnson, D. W. (2015). What conditions support safety in urban schools? The influence of school organizational practices on student and teacher reports of safety in Chicago. In D. Losen (Ed.), *Closing the school discipline gap: Equitable remedies for excessive exclusion* (pp. 118–131). Teachers College Press.

Subramanian, S. V., Belli, P., & Kawachi, I. (2002). The macroeconomic determinants of health. *Annual Review of Public Health, 23*(1), 287–302. https://doi.org/10.1146/annurev.publhealth.23.100901.140540

Sugai, G., & Horner, R. (2002). The evolution of discipline practices: School-wide positive behavior supports. *Child and Family Behavior Therapy, 24*(1/2), 23–50. https://doi.org/10.1300/J019v24n01_03

Sutcher, L., Darling-Hammond, L., & Carver-Thomas, D. (2016). *A coming crisis in teaching? Teacher supply, demand, and shortages in the U.S.* Learning Policy Institute. https://doi.org/10.54300/247.242

Swanson, C. B. (2004). Sketching a portrait of public high school graduation: Who graduates? Who doesn't? In Orfield, G. (Ed.), *Dropouts in America: Confronting the graduation rate crisis* (pp. 13–40). Harvard Education Press.

Szmigiera, M. (2021). *Child poverty in OECD countries, 2019.* Statista. https://www .statista.com/statistics/264424/child-poverty-in-oecd-countries/

Tankersley, J., Sanger-Katz, M., Rappeport, A., & Cochrane, E. (2020, February 10). Trump's $4.8 trillion budget would cut safety net programs and boost defense. *The New York Times.* https://www.nytimes.com/2020/02/10/business/president-trump -budget-cuts.html

Tate, E. (2019, May). Why social–emotional learning is suddenly in the spotlight. *Ed-Surge Podcast.* https://www.edsurge.com/news/2019-05-07-why-social-emotional -learning-is-suddenly-in-the-spotlight

Taylor, R. D., Oberle, E., Durlak, J. A., & Weissberg, R. P. (2017). Promoting positive youth development through school-based social and emotional learning interventions: A meta-analysis of follow-up effects. *Child Development, 88*(4), 1156–1171. https://doi.org/10.1111/cdev.12864

Terman, L. M., Dickson, V. E., Sutherland, A. H., Franzen, R. H., Tupper, C. R., & Fernald, G. (1922). *Intelligence Tests and School Reorganization.* World Book Company.

Theriot, M. T., & Dupper, D. R. (2010). Student discipline problems and the transition from elementary to middle school. *Education and Urban Society, 42,* 205–222. https://doi.org/10.1177/0013124509349583v

Thompson, C. (2021). *Felicitas & Gonzalo Mendez High School: A community school that honors its neighborhood's legacy of educational justice.* Learning Policy Institute. https://learningpolicyinstitute.org/product/shared-learning-mendez-brief

Thurlow, M. L., Sinclair, M. F., & Johnson, D. R. (2002). *Students with disabilities who drop out of school: Implications for policy and practice.* Institute on Community Integration, National Center on Secondary Education and Transition, University of Minnesota

Tyack, D. B. (1974). *The one best system: A history of American urban education.* Harvard University Press.

United States Courts. (n.d.). History—*Brown v. Board of Education* re-enactment. https://www.uscourts.gov/educational-resources/educational-activities/history -brown-v-board-education-re-enactment

U.S. Bureau of Labor Statistics. (2022, April 18). *Occupational outlook handbook: Fastest growing occupations.* https://www.bls.gov/ooh/fastest-growing.htm

U.S. Census Bureau. (2012). *Current population survey, annual social and economic supplement.* https://www2.census.gov/programs-surveys/cps/techdocs/cpsmar12 .pdf

U.S. Commission on Civil Rights. (2013). *School discipline and disparate impact: A briefing before the United States Commission on Civil Rights held in Washington, DC* [Briefing report]. Author. https://www.usccr.gov/files/pubs/docs/School _Disciplineand_Disparate_Impact.pdf

U.S. Commission on Civil Rights. (2019). *Beyond suspensions: Examining school discipline policies and connections to the school-to-prison pipeline for students of color with disabilities* [Briefing report]. https://www.usccr.gov/pubs/2019/07 -23-Beyond-Suspensions.pdf

U.S. Department of Commerce, Bureau of the Census. *Historical poverty tables: People and families, 1959–2020.* https://www.census.gov/data/tables/time-series /demo/income-poverty/historical-poverty-people.html

U.S. Department of Education. (2013). *For each and every child: A strategy for education equity and excellence.* https://oese.ed.gov/files/2020/10/equity-excellence-commission-report.pdf

U.S. Department of Education. (2015). *School climate and discipline: Federal efforts.* https://www2.ed.gov/policy/gen/guid/school-discipline/fedefforts.html

U.S. Department of Education Office for Civil Rights. (2016). *2013–2014 civil rights data collection. A first look: Key data highlights on equity and opportunity gaps in our nation's public schools.* https://www2.ed.gov/about/offices/list/ocr/docs/2013-14-first-look.pdf

U.S. Department of Education Office for Civil Rights. (2021). *Civil rights data collection, 2017–18 state and national estimations.* https://ocrdata.ed.gov/estimations/2017-2018

U.S. Department of Justice, Civil Rights Division, & U.S. Department of Education Office for Civil Rights. (2014, January 8). *Dear Colleague letter on the nondiscriminatory administration of school discipline.*

Valencia, R. R. (2005). The Mexican American struggle for equal educational opportunity in Mendez v. Westminster: Helping to pave the way for Brown v. Board of Education. *Teachers College Record, 107*(3), 389–423.

Vogel, S., & Schwabe, L. (2016). Learning and memory under stress: Implications for the classroom. *Science of Learning, 1*(16011). https://doi.org/10.1038/npjscilearn.2016.11

Voight, A., Hanson, T., O'Malley, M., & Adekanye, L. (2015). The racial school climate gap: Within-school disparities in students' experiences of safety, support, and connectedness. *American Journal of Community Psychology, 56*(3–4), 252–267. https://doi.org/10.1007/s10464-015-9751-x

Volsky, I. (2014, January 8). *Racism, sexism, and the 50-year campaign to undermine the War on Poverty.* ThinkProgress. https://archive.thinkprogress.org/racism-sexism-and-the-50-year-campaign-to-undermine-the-war-on-poverty-452430bff8ad/

Wald, J., & Losen, D. (2003). Defining and redirecting a school-to-prison pipeline. *New Directions for Youth Development, 99*, 9–15. https://doi.org/10.1002/yd.51

Weiss, D. C. (2017, January 31). Class action filed on behalf of Flint residents claims EPA negligence in water probe. *ABA Journal Daily News.* https://www.abajournal.com/news/article/class_action_filed_on_behalf_of_flint_residents_claims_epa_negligence_in_wa

Wells, A. S., Fox, L., & Cordova-Cobo, D. (2016). *Research fact sheet: The educational benefits of diverse schools and classrooms for all students.* American Educational Research Association.

WestEd. (2019). *Sound basic education for all: An action plan for North Carolina.* https://www.ednc.org/wp-content/uploads/2020/02/Sound-Basic-Education-for-All-An-Action-Plan-for-North-Carolina.pdfH

Whisman, A., & Hammer, P. C. (2014). *The association between school discipline and mathematics performance: A case for positive discipline approaches.* Division of Teaching and Learning Office of Research, West Virginia Department of Education. https://files.eric.ed.gov/fulltext/ED569903.pdf

Williams v. State of California, Superior Court of the State of CA for the County of San Francisco, 2001, Complaint.

Wise, A. E. (1965). Is denial of equal educational opportunity constitutional? *Administrator's Notebook, 13*(6), 1–4.

Worrell, F. C., Olszewski-Kubilius, P., & Subotnik, R. F. (2012, November 2). Where are the gifted minorities?. *Scientific American Blog*. https://blogs.scientificamerican.com/streams-of-consciousness/where-are-the-gifted-minorities/

Yuan, K., & Le, V.-H. (2012). *Estimating the percentage of students who were tested on cognitively demanding items through the state achievement tests*. RAND Corporation. https://www.rand.org/pubs/working_papers/WR967.html.

Zhu, B., Gnedko-Berry, N., Borman, T., & Manzeske, D. (2019). *Effects of National Board Certified instructional leaders on classroom practice and student achievement of novice teachers*. American Institutes of Research.

Index

The letters *f* and *t* after a page number indicate a figure or table, respectively.

Mentoring of teachers, 69–70, 72
Mercer, C., 75n11
Merrill, L., 66n13
Mexican Americans, 25, 26, 29, 65, 69, 81.
    See also Race/ethnicity
Michael, R. S., 45n32
Michigan in the World and the
    Environmental Justice HistoryLab,
    22n55
Mickelson, R. A., 11n13, 12n19, 35n33,
    36n34, 82n28
Midtown West Elementary School, 3–6, 60
Milam, A. J., 21n49
Milem, J. F., 81n25
Milliken v. Bradley, 29
Millman, O., 13n1
Mitchell, B., 50n57
Mitchell, C., 19n40
Mixed-age groups, 7–8
Monitoring of expulsions and suspensions, 54
Moore, H., 40n8
Morello-Frosch, R., 14n10, 14n11, 14n12,
    14n13, 14n14, 15n15
Morning meetings, 43–44
Morris, E. W., 47n46
Mortenson, E., 45n30
Mortgage risk assessment and redlining,
    20–21
Mourshed, M., 59n1
Multilingual students, 6–7, 52

NAEP (National Assessment of Educational
    Progress), 34, 69
Nakasato, J., 50n53
Nance, J. P., 47n43, 55n65
Nardo, A. C., 45n32
National Assessment of Educational Progress
    (NAEP), 26f, 34, 69
National Education Association, 48n51
National Education Goals Panel, 68–69, 70,
    70n33
National Research Council, 70n33
National School Climate Center, 40, 40n7, 41
National Scientific Council on the Developing
    Child, 40n4, 41n12
Nation's Report Card, 26f
Native Americans, 45. *See also* Race/ethnicity
Native language, 7
NCLB (No Child Left Behind), 19, 74–75, 83
Neighborhood violence, 21, 22
Nelson, C. M., 50n57
Nelson, L., 19n35, 19n37, 19n38

Neurodevelopmental Center of Excellence,
    17–18
New Jersey and school funding, 30–32,
    33–34, 35
New York State school funding, 70
New York Times, 17
Nguyen-Hoang, P., 34n28
Nixon Administration, 29, 36
Nkomo, M., 11n13, 12n19
No Child Left Behind (NCLB), 19, 74–75,
    83
Noguera, P. A., 73n2, 75n9, 76n21
Nonrepresentation, 45
Normalcy beliefs, 45
Norrington-Sands, K., 21n50
Nuñez Estrada, J., 41n13

Oakes, J., 3–5, 44n26, 51n60, 60n2,
    60n3, 61–64, 66n16, 67n20, 70n33,
    74n6
Oakland International High School, 51–54
Oakland Technical High School, 52
Oakland Unified School District, 79
Obama Administration, 36, 54, 56
Oberle, E., 11n18
Office of Special Education Programs
    Technical Assistance Center, 50n57
Office of the Assistant Secretary for Planning
    and Education, 25n68
Ogden, L. A., 20n43
Olszewski-Kubilius, P., 73n2
O'Malley, M., 45n29
O'Neil-Dunne, J. P., 20n43
Opening Doors, Expanding Opportunities,
    12n22
Orfield, G., 29n10, 36n36, 36n37
Osher, D., 21n48, 39n2, 43n21, 48n50

Pachan, M., 11n18
Pacific Islander. *See* Race/ethnicity
Padres and Jovenes Unidos, 41n11, 47n41,
    47n42, 47n43
Page, S., 12n19
*Parents Involved in Community Schools v.
    Seattle School District No 1.*, 36n38, 37
Parolin, Z., 26n73
Pastor, M., 14n10, 14n11, 14n12, 14n13,
    14n14, 15n15
Patricia (teacher), 6–8
Payton, J., 11n18
PCBs (polychlorinated biphenyls) landfill, 23
Pendleton, N., 20n44

Penner, E. K., 81n24
Perez, T., 12
Perry, B. L., 47n46
Persico, C., 35n31
Persistent traumatic stress environments (PTSEs), 21
Personalized learning experience, 68, 69, 76, 78–79
Personal Responsibility and Work Opportunity Reconciliation Act, 25
Persson, H., 50n54
Peterson, R. D., 21n49
Peterson, R. L., 45n32
Petrosino, A., 50n54
Pickett, S. T., 20n43
Pillsbury, W. B., 74n5
PISA (Program for International Student Assessment), 81
Plessy v. Ferguson, 10
Plotkin, M., 47n40, 47n42, 47n43, 47n44
Podolsky, A., 65n7, 72n36
Policy coordination, 84
Pollen, T., 3–6, 60
Polychlorinated biphenyls (PCBs) landfill, 23
Poole, M. K., 19n39
Pootinath, P., 82n29
Poverty, 13–14, 15, 19–20, 24–26, 29, 75, 85
Prados, M. J.,75n14
Preschool, 46, 75–76, 85
Principal Fellows program, 68
Professional learning opportunities, 67–68, 76, 88–89
Professional standards for teaching, 56, 66, 69, 88
Program for International Student Assessment (PISA), 81
Progressive funding systems, 29, 34
Property tax funding systems, 65–66, 68
Prucha, F. P., 10n10
Pryiomka, K., 81n23
PTSEs (persistent traumatic stress environments), 21
Pulido, L., 14n11
Putman, B., 50n57

Qualifications for teaching. *See* Teachers: professional standards
Quality of curriculum. *See* High-quality curriculum
Quality of teaching. *See* High-quality teaching
Quintana, C., 48

Race/ethnicity
- academic achievement, 19, 25, 26*f*, 29, 35–36, 65, 69, 81
- and erasure, 45
- exclusionary discipline, 44–48, 54–55, 57, 65
- historical school exclusion, 9–11, 20–21, 73–74
- and poverty, 13–14, 25, 26*f*
- residential policies, 20–21
- school curriculum, 73–74, 77, 81
- school funding, 28–29, 36–37
- segregation, 10, 28, 29, 30*f*, 36, 37–38, 74
- slavery, 9–10, 73
- and toxic environments, 14–15, 19–21, 23–24
- whole-child approach, 37–38

Race representation and teaching corps, 11, 66
Rafa, A., 56n70
Raffaele Mendez, L. M., 45n30
Rappeport, A., 24n62
Rausch, M. K., 47n46
Reagan Administration, 10, 25, 36
Reardon, S., 30*f*, 65n7
Recruitment incentives, 72, 88
Redding, C., 73n2
Redfield, S. E., 47n43, 55n65
Redlining, 20–21
Relationships, 4, 39, 41, 44, 48, 49, 53–54, 86
Resegregation, 36
Residential policies, 20–21
Restorative deans, 49
Restorative practices, 48–50, 56, 57, 58
Reyes, C. R., 47n36
Reynolds, L., 16n23
Richardson, N., 78–80
Ritter, G., 47n46
Roberts v. City of Boston, 10
Robinson, K. J., 82n31
Robinson v. Cahill, 30
Roc, M., 6–9, 75n11
Rockoff, J., 70n32
Rogers, B., 48–50, 81n23
Ronfeldt, M., 66n13, 66n14
Rose, J., 45n32
Rose, S. J., 1n2
Rose, T., 39n2
Ross, P., 6–9
Rothstein, E., 16n23
Rothstein, R., 13n4, 13n6

About the Authors

Kia Darling-Hammond is author of the *Bridge to Thriving Framework©* and CEO of Wise Chipmunk LLC, an education and research firm that advises and supports learning opportunities for students, educators, organizations, and policymakers. These have included the Congressional Black Mental Health Brain Trust and the Congressional Black Caucus's Suicide Prevention Taskforce, whose work advanced the *Pursuing Equity in Mental Health Act.*

Linda Darling-Hammond is the Charles E. Ducommun Professor of Education Emeritus at Stanford University and founding president of the Learning Policy Institute. She is past president of the American Educational Research Association and author of more than 30 books and 700 other publications on teaching quality, school reform, and educational equity, including *The Flat World and Education: How America's Commitment to Equity Will Determine Our Future,* which won the Grawemeyer Award in 2010. In 2006, *Education Week* named her one of the nation's 10 most influential people affecting educational policy. She led the Obama education policy transition team in 2008 and the Biden education transition team in 2020. She currently serves as president of California's State Board of Education.